THE AUSTRALIAN
AND OTHER VERSES

THE AUSTRALIAN
AND OTHER VERSES
BY
WILL H. OGILVIE

Angus & Robertson Publishers

THE AUSTRALIAN

AND OTHER VERSES

BY
WILL H. OGILVIE
Author of "Fair Girls and Gray Horses" and "Hearts of Gold"

Angus & Robertson Publishers

ANGUS & ROBERTSON PUBLISHERS
London • Sydney • Melbourne • Singapore • Manila

This book is copyright. Apart from any fair dealing for the purposes of private study, research, criticism or review, as permitted under the Copyright Act, no part may be reproduced by any process without written permission. Inquiries should be addressed to the publishers.

First published by Angus & Robertson Publishers, Australia, 1916
This edition 1982

Copyright G. A. Ogilvie, 1916

National Library of Australia
Cataloguing-in-publication data.

Ogilvie, Will, 1869–1963.
   The Australian and other verses.

   First published: Sydney: Angus & Robertson, 1916.
   ISBN 0 207 14547 4.

   I. Title.

A821'.2

Printed in Hong Kong

To
THE MEN
OF AUSTRALIA,
who have proved for all time their
unconquerable spirit and unswerving loyalty to
the right, I dedicate these songs of
the misty land they fought for
and the sunny land
that bred them

The verses from which this volume takes its title—*The Australian*—first appeared in London *Punch*. Other pieces have appeared in the *Spectator, Bulletin, Lone Hand, Pall Mall Magazine, Glasgow Herald, Westminster Gazette, British Australasian* and *Scotsman*. My thanks are due to the Proprietors for permission to reprint.

W. H. O.

CONTENTS

THE AUSTRALIAN

	Page
THE AUSTRALIAN	
The skies that arched his land were blue ...	3

SUNNY COUNTRY

SUNNY COUNTRY	
I dreamed of Sunny Country last night, a golden dream ...	7
THE BUSHMEN	
God, the day He fashioned them ..	8
THE OVERLANDER	
I knew them on the road: red, roan, and white ...	10
THE RIDING CAMEL	
I was Junda's riding camel. I went in front of the train ...	16

CONTENTS

	Page
A LEAF FROM MACQUARIE A gumleaf from Warren, all withered and brown . . .	21
MY AUSTRALIAN SPURS Old and worn my Bushland spurs . . .	23
THE OUTLAW Our realm was the fenceless ranges. We fed in the bluegrass swamps . . .	25
THE PACK HORSE My hoofs were hid by the dew-wet clover . . .	30
THE WHITE IBIS When the fierce Barwon from the Border brings . . .	34
CICADAS When the Bush is still as death . .	36
SYDNEY The green Bush mantles your shoulder . . .	38
A BUSH NIGHT I remember the tilt on the deep canvas chairs, and the men sitting idle . . .	40
THE AUSTRALIAN FLEET Long and long has she slumbered, till many a mouth denied . . .	42

CONTENTS

	Page
BLACK WINGS Sextons of the Overland! Buriers of the dead . .	44
THE TEAM BULLOCK The sunrays scorched like furnace fires . . .	46
BLACK TRACKERS Swart bloodhounds of the fenceless West . . .	50
COO-EE! Foam that feeds the Leeuwin . . .	52
COMRADES Do the shearers still go riding up the Warrego to work . . .	54
THE BUSH I hear you slighted often and maligned . . .	56

STEEDS OF THE MIST

STEEDS OF THE MIST Steeds, O Steeds of the morning mist . . .	59
THE WHAUP This is the lark of the hilltops . . .	61

CONTENTS

	Page
THE INGLESIDE	
When the shadows downward glide . . .	63
THE HORSEMAN	
My song is of the Horseman—who woke the world's unrest . . .	65
THE SIGNPOST	
On my green grass plot I stand aloof . . .	67
A SONG OF THE POETS	
Bridges, Abercrombie, Davies . . .	70
THE GIPSY	
"Now cross my hand with silver" said the gipsy crone to me . . .	72
THE FLYING SCOTSMAN	
'Tis ten o'clock at King's Cross. A green flag flicks the air . . .	74
LAST NIGHT	
Last night I heard as in a dream . . .	76
THE CARPET OF THE WIND	
In the deep of the woodland places . . .	78
CELANDINE	
You blossom in no garden fair . . .	80

CONTENTS

	Page
LAUGHTER	
Lend us Laughter, O gods, for our life is but vain	81
AGAIN	
Ain't it good to see again . . .	82
BY CANDLE-LIGHT	
I went with my love by candle-light through the deep of the poplar grove. . .	84
THE GARDEN OF NIGHT	
The Night is a far spreading garden, and all through the hours . . .	86
THE MUSHROOM GATHERERS	
Ere Fashion has waked to adorning . . .	88
THE BORDER HARP	
Lilting ballads there are that cling . . .	90
A LITTLE BIT OF GARDEN	
We need no crown or sceptre . . .	92
A FAREWELL	
Flowers in my fading garden . . .	94
THERE'S A CLEAN WIND BLOWING	
There's a clean wind blowing . . .	96
SHEEP COUNTRY	
Flame of the heather dying . . .	98

CONTENTS

	Page
THE PLOUGH	
From Egypt behind my oxen with their stately step and slow . . .	100
THE COMFORT OF THE HILLS	
Heart! If you've a sorrow . . .	103
THE ROMAN WALL	
The grey moor dips to the mist-blue valley . . .	105
THE SHADOW DANCERS	
When the swallow's dipping low and the cloud's above the wheat . . .	107
FLOWERS OF THE FROST	
The sun is a king on the crest of the hill . . .	108
CONTENTMENT	
The gold leaf said to the brown . . .	110
RICHES	
I may neither sport nor feast . . .	111
THE BROWN MEN	
Lean men, brown men, men from overseas . . .	113
A MAKER OF EMPIRE	
A patient, honest, kindly friend . . .	114
A SUMMER EVENING	
Dusk o' the night comes down like wings . . .	116

CONTENTS

Page

THE HAPPY PEOPLE

THE HAPPY PEOPLE
    Do you know the Happy People? The really happy folk . . .   119

A LULLABY
    Lady Moon, O Lady Moon . . .   121

THE ADMIRAL
    Low in his cushions, with wide blue eyes . . .   123

THE BRINGER OF DAYS
    There are far places where she plays . . .   125

THREE
    Up at seven and down the stair . . .   126

BABY'S TRUMPET
    When Baby blows her trumpet . . .   127

THE GREY NURSE
    At the feet of this oldest of nurses . . .   129

THE BURNING OF SUMMER
    I heard a laugh in the leafless trees . . .   131

A SONG OF THE RAIN
    The rain swept over the hill . . .   132

CONTENTS

	Page
THE BUNDLE IN THE SHAWL In all the sorrow of the street . . .	133
TO MY BABY GIRL O, little heart . .	135
IN THE WOODS The North winds blow with a promise of snow . . .	136
THE WITCHES' STEEDS There are four wild steeds that the witches ride . . .	138
THE BARRING OF THE GATES The Fairy King lies dead.—Ring, ring the bluebells over him! . . .	140
THE STORKS There's a quaint old Nor'land fancy and a legend that I love . . .	142

WAR!

A DREAM OF ENGLAND I dreamed a dream . . .	145
WAR War! The winds are sighing it . . .	147

CONTENTS

	Page
A SONG OF THE OLD MEN	
Youth! To you is the splendid prize ...	149
THE STRAGGLERS	
Under the blue of wide heavens in the haze of the Western heat ...	150
THE CHANNEL GUARD	
Where runs the Channel East and West ...	152
A BEGGING SONG FOR BELGIUM	
Here's a beggar, here's a gipsy, here's a tramp ...	154
THE UNAWAKENED HILLS	
Here, in the unawakened hills ...	156
THE LADIES FROM HELL	
The battle sways backward and forward ...	158
O WEEPING GLENS!	
O weeping glens; O mountain peaks that mourn ...	160
THE SCOTS GREYS	
O "terrible grey horses" that woke Napoleon's fears	161
THE COLOURS	
In this dim Cathedral place ...	162
REMOUNTS	
In the rosy red of the dawning your hoofs on the roadway ring ...	164

CONTENTS

	Page
THE HEROES	
There came a west wind swinging . . .	166
SAILS OF VICTORY	
Where the lone look-outs their night-watch keep . . .	169
A SONG OF THE FLAG	
There's a flag the free winds follow—'tis the banner England bought her . . .	170

The Australian

The Australian

"The bravest thing God ever made"—
A British Officer's opinion.

The skies that arched his land were blue,
  His bush-born winds were warm and sweet,
And yet from earliest hours he knew
  The tides of victory and defeat;
From fierce floods thundering at his birth,
  From red droughts ravening while he played,
He learned to fear no foes on earth—
  "The bravest thing God ever made!"

The bugles of the Motherland
  Rang ceaselessly across the sea,
To call him and his lean brown band
  To shape Imperial destiny;
He went, by youth's grave purpose willed,
  The goal unknown, the cost unweighed,
The promise of his blood fulfilled—
  "The bravest thing God ever made!"

THE AUSTRALIAN

We know—it is our deathless pride!—
  The splendour of his first fierce blow;
How, reckless, glorious, undenied,
  He stormed those steel-lined cliffs we know!
And none who saw him scale the height
  Behind his reeking bayonet-blade
Would rob him of his title-right—
  "The bravest thing God ever made!"

Bravest, where half a world of men
  Are brave beyond all earth's rewards,
So stoutly none shall charge again
  Till the last breaking of the swords;
Wounded or hale, won home from war,
  Or yonder by the Lone Pine laid,
Give him his due for evermore—
  "The bravest thing God ever made!"

Sunny Country

Sunny Country

I dreamed of Sunny Country last night, a golden dream
Of wattles down the gully and of gum trees by the stream,
Of dancing haze and skies of blue no other land can show
Save this—our Sunny Country, where the golden wattles grow.

I dreamed of Sunny Country; a dream-ship took me down
Far out of misty Scotland and the fogs of London town;
My foot was on the stirrup-bar; down bridle-tracks of old
I rode through Sunny Country in a blaze of blue and gold.

I woke again to labour; all day the skies of blue
Have roofed my house of fancy, and the sun has warmed me
    through,
And if the days are dark and drear, the sweeter sleeptime seems
When I sail to Sunny Country in my white-winged ship of
    dreams.

The Bushmen

God, the day He fashioned them,
  Toiled to make them true,
Hand and head and heart of them,
  Blood and bone and thew;
Set them in the foremost rank
  Giants' work to do.

God, the day He fashioned them,
  Bred them to their sires,
Supple as their bullock-whips,
  Tough as twisted wires,
Filled the sturdy brains of them
  With His battle-fires.

Then when He had fashioned them,
  Tried them for His pride,
Sent His droughts and chastened them,
  Sent His flames to chide,
Sent His floods to harry them
  Wasting far and wide.

THE BUSHMEN

But the strength He set in them
  Braced His fighting brood,
Bravely, face to face with Him,
  Shoulder-firm they stood—
Then the God who fashioned them
  Knew His work was good!

So, when He has gathered them,
  God will not forget;
High at the right hand of Him
  He shall have them set;
Paying thus for pride of them
  Seven-fold His debt!

The Overlander

I knew them on the road: red, roan, and white,
  Cock-horned and spear-horned, spotted, streaked and starred;
I knew their shapes moon-misted in the night
  As I rode round them keeping lonely guard.
I knew them all, the laggards and the leaders,
The wild, the wandering, and the listless feeders.

And when I, weary, by the camp-fire slept,
  Booted and spurred, beneath Heaven's rafter beams,
With slow and measured step their hundreds kept
  Moving and moving past me in my dreams.
I knew them all: streaked, spotted, roan and red;
A thousand steers, range-run and Queensland bred.

I loved the wide gold glitter of the plains
  Spread out before us like a silent sea,
The lazy lapping of the loose-held reins,
  The sense of motion and of mystery
As the great beasts slid slowly through the grass,
One passing one, then letting it re-pass.

THE OVERLANDER

I loved the misty sunrise, when the herd
  Drew from the camp, close-ranked, with clash of horn.
When 'neath their hoofs the scented dust was stirred
  Still heavy with the dew-fall of the morn.
I loved the jingle of the swaying load
As the lean pack-horse lobbed into the road.

So, day by day, as men have done for years,
  Across the plain we brought the cattle down;
And half my heart was with the moving steers
  And half lay yonder in a Border town;
For, waiting there, my guerdon and my prize,
Was home, and love, and little Laughing Eyes.

I was a western bushman born and bred,
  And so I loved the cattle, as men do
Whose life is to the dusty sandhills wed,
  Whose world is bounded by a fence of blue;
Yet one flower nearer to my heart I wore—
The baby laughter of a child of four.

The lories screamed above us as we rode;
  The emus ran before us, swift with fear.
A great resistless tide of life we flowed,
  The largest mob out of the north that year;
The muffled moving of the many feet
Like sighing waves upon the silence beat.

THE OVERLANDER

Two hundred leagues of stock-route burnt and brown
   In twelve-mile stages day by dazzling day
Had worn the cleft hoofs of our cattle down,
   But had not stolen their wild hearts away;
And in wide eyes, 'neath shaggy frontlets set,
The fire of the free ranges smouldered yet.

A swagman stumbling down the dusty track,
   His blanket bundle on his shoulder borne,
Would send the startled flankers rushing back
   To stop and stare at him, with tossing horn.
A camel train across the sandhill stringing
Would lift all heads and set the leaders ringing.

At night a blown bough tapping on the wire
   Would bring them scared and restless to their feet;
A burnt log crashing inward on the fire
   Would lash their rebel blood to fever heat;
And on the stormier nights when winds blew hard
'Twas double watch—and sometimes three on guard.

As we drew near the Border, tank and creek
   For water failed us, and stage after stage
The poor brutes plodded on for near a week
   In thirst that we were powerless to assuage.
Blind, dropping froth, they stumbled in their going
And filled the sandhills with their piteous lowing.

THE OVERLANDER

On all the earth there is no sadder sound
   Than moan of cattle when their thirst is great;
It quivers in the trees, and sky and ground
   With all its hopelessness reverberate:
This heart-cry of the dumb brutes in the wild
That sears you like the sobbing of a child.

We hung our stock whips on our saddle-dees;
   We crooned to the great beasts to soothe their pain;
We sang to them to set them at their ease;
   But still their weird, low moaning filled the plain,
As, blind, they passed us on their ceaseless quest,
Pleading for water till the suns went west.

We reached the Border. On the night before,
   Forgetting for an hour those moaning cries,
I found again the little flower I wore
   Close to my heart, and dreamed of Laughing Eyes.
Ere the next night should come with star flag streaming
My arms should hold her: so I thought of dreaming.

The cattle passed the netting fence at noon.
   Day blazed upon the glittering township roofs.
The sun peered like a pale and misty moon
   Through the red dust wrack of the drumming hoofs.
They smelt the water at the dams already;
We rode in front to hold the leaders steady.

THE OVERLANDER

Voices they heard not; whips they would not heed.
    They swept upon us like a tide-wave's flow.
The dust rose up and wrapped us, man and steed;
    And through the dust came thrilling—"Let them go!"—
Swift towards the gleam that marked the river bed,
Mad, blind, unbound, thundered the thousand head.

The red earth shook. The horns flashed by like flame.
    The moaning rose and gathered to a roar.
All passed; even the laggard and the lame;
    The plain lay empty as a desolate shore.
A known roof glimmered under dust-brown skies!
Home!—Home at last, and love—and Laughing Eyes!

Behind the mob the dust clouds thinned and cleared,
    And as the sun broke through with sudden light
A tiny heap upon the sand appeared,
    A heap of white: a—huddled—heap—of—white!
Ah! God!—I live again that anguished hour!
The tattered, trampled thing!—My flower! my flower!

    .   .   .   .   .   .

All day I see them moving, moving by;
    All night I hear them moaning in my dreams.

THE OVERLANDER

Always that little heap—ah! let it lie!—
  Always the dust that whirls, the roof that gleams!
Always the sunlight as the dust clouds part,
And shadow, shadow, shadow on my heart!

The city reels about me. Carts and cars
  Make thunder down the streetways east and west,
But out amid the silence and the stars
  I ride around my cattle as they rest.
The camp fire's banners on the dark extend;
The horse bells jangle in the river bend.

The grey dawns wake them; out of sleep they start,
  And draw amid the dim light down the plain;
Their every hoof is heavy on my heart,
  Their every horn stabs deep with an old pain;
And yet I love my cattle—God knows why!—
I sing to them, I sing as they go by.

I know them all so well; red, roan, and white,
  Cock-horned and curly, spotted, streaked and starred;
I know their shapes moon-marked upon the night
  As I ride round them keeping lonely guard.
I love them all: streaked, spotted, roan and red;
My thousand steers, range-run and Queensland bred.

The Riding Camel

I was Junda's riding camel. I went in front of the train.
I was hung with shells of the Orient, from saddle and cinch
 and rein.
I was sour as a snake to handle, and rough as a rock to ride,
But I could keep up with the west wind, and my pace was
 Junda's pride.

I was Junda's riding camel. When first we left our land
Camels were rare on the Queensland tracks as ropes made out
 of the sand;
But slowly we conquered a kingdom till down through the dust
 and heat
Not a road from the Gulf to the Border but carried the print
 of our feet.

And I was the riding camel. I carried him—Junda Khan—
The dark-skinned Afghan devil made in the mould of a man!
I gave no service to others, yellow, or white, or brown,
But Junda Khan was my master; I knelt when he "Hooshed!"
 me down.

THE RIDING CAMEL

When the gloom on his forehead gathered, when he fingered the blade at his belt,
The men who handled the nose-strings knelt low as the camels knelt;
For each of them—beast and driver—from Koot to the camel-foal,
Knew that the man who led them owned them body and soul.

Northward I carried my master. The creek by the road was dry;
The sun like a burning waggon-wheel rolled down in the western sky;
The dust was white on the saltbush, the ruts were deep in the road,
And the camel behind me grunted at every lurch of his load.

A dust-whirl rose in the bushes and circled into the sky,
The shells on my harness rattled as its burning breath went by.
And out of the endless distance clear-cut on the world's edge lone
Like a silver sail on the ocean the roof of a homestead shone.

The white man stood at my shoulder, sunburnt, lissome and straight,
In the deep of his eyes was anger to match with the Afghan's hate.

THE RIDING CAMEL

I know no word of the quarrel. The "Hoosh-ta!" came and I knelt;
And Junda sprang from my saddle, and the knife leapt out of his belt.

There was a cry in the sunset, an echo that rang at the ford;
Then silence fell on the roadway till a scared bull-camel roared.
My master turned and mounted; I felt the sting of his goad,
And we swept away through the saltbush; and the rest stood still on the road.

The night came up from the river, darksome and deep and drear.
Swift were my feet on the sandhill, but swifter followed his fear.
When the stars were dim in the daylight and the moon on the mulga low
A hundred miles of desert lay between the blade and the blow.

We were far from the fetter of fences and far from the dwellings of men,
Yet for less than an hour he rested, then mounted and rode again.
I was sore and weary and thirsty when out of the blaze of noon
We camped in the shade of a wilga clump and drank at a long lagoon.

THE RIDING CAMEL

Ah! Never was life-blood taken of white, or yellow, or brown
But the keen-eyed men in the helmets have ridden the taker down!
Never a trail on the sandhill of camel, or horse, or shoe
Crossed by a hundred others but the trackers have tracked it through!

Sore of the saddle and weary, Junda, the killer, slept;
But I, I watched from the bushes while the armed avenger crept.
Sharp came the call in the English tongue, and my master sprang from sleep,
Hand to the hilt of his Khyber knife, crouched for his one swift leap.

Brave are these outpost English, but simple as children be;
The pistol-barrel that held his life hung loose at the trooper's knee.
There was a flash in the sunlight, the gleam of a long blue blade,
A cry in the noontide stillness, a corpse on the sandhill laid.

I was his riding camel; but deep in my heart there stirred
Something of lust and anger I could not name in a word.
When he came to me swift and sudden, the blood-red knife in his belt,
I could not kneel at his bidding as I and my sires had knelt.

THE RIDING CAMEL

Wrath at his long-time goading, fear of his cruel hand,
Made me a raging devil that heard no man's command.
And when he struck at my nostrils, mad with his human fear,
I clenched my teeth in his shoulder, and clung till the blood ran clear.

I knelt with my weight and crushed him. He died, and at Allah's Gate
The soul of him sobs and trembles where the grim Black Camels wait.
Could I do else, my brothers, I who remembered then
The moan of the laden pack-beasts and the mutter of Junda's men?

A Leaf from Macquarie

A gumleaf from Warren, all withered and brown,
  Fluttered out from a letter to-day,
And my heart has gone back where Macquarie winds
    down
By dusty red stock-route and sleepy grey town
  Between banks where the river-oaks sway.

The far-travelled sheep lie at rest in the bend,
  And the camp fire gleams red to the sky,
The shadows creep round us, and day's at an end
And the gum trees lean down to us, friend unto friend,
  As the night-winds go murmuring by.

Not a horse-bell of ours but the gum trees have heard
  As their watch by our camp fire they keep;
Not a tired overlander, stretched, booted and spurred.
In a dream of mobs rushing has muttered and stirred
  But the gums sang him back to his sleep.

A LEAF FROM MACQUARIE

Aye! and those of us holding lone watch in the night—
   Have we ever looked upward in vain
To the magic brown branches that trellis the blue,
Where the stars of our comfort look hopefully through,
   Giving strength for the battle again.

A leaf from Macquarie! My heart's on the road
   With a mob yarded out of the years!
No higher-prized gift could a hand have bestowed
Than this withered brown leaf with its mystical load
   Of old laughter, old labour, and tears!

My Australian Spurs

Old and worn my Bushland spurs
   Hang above my desk to-day.
Memory, on that broom of hers,
   Witchlike bears my heart away
Over seas that restless roll,
   'Neath forgotten stars that shine,
To a dim and distant goal
   In a land that once was mine.

There I wake where Dawn has trod,
   Bind again those friends of steel,
As the happy morning god
   Binds the sunlight on his heel,
Taking back on golden plains
   Youth set free of Time's reproofs,
Laughter loosening the reins,
   Joy that speeds the lifting hoofs.

MY AUSTRALIAN SPURS

Gathering from the morning mist
  Come the comrades loved of old,
Brown of cheek and red of wrist,
  And with hearts of royal gold,
Iron-thighed and lithe and lean,
  Toilers of the rope and brand,
Men who know what friendships mean
  And the worth of hand on hand.

Through the drowsy Bush we ride
  (Lonely, worn Australian spurs!)—
Half the world can ne'er divide
  These our exiled hearts from hers!
From her gum-trees' chequered shade,
  From her rivers brown and low,
From the call our hearts obeyed
  Long, and long, and long ago!

Better far that yonder wall
  Keep my old Australian spurs,
If it be the Bushland call
  Now no more our troop bestirs;
But if gay they gather yet
  Where the scrub-line meets the blue,
When your broom is Southward set,
  Witch, take back my heart with you!

The Outlaw

Our realm was the fenceless ranges. We fed in the bluegrass swamps.
The green of the branching wilga was the roof of our noon-day camps.
We drank at the pools in the lignum, where the mist and moonlight meet,
Stealing like wraiths through the darkness with the dew on our shoeless feet.

I was the chief and warden. I watched while the shy mares fed.
I herded the bitless yearlings—those proud, wild sons I bred.
When a dry twig snapped in the forest, when a snake slid out of the grass,
I called my mob together till I saw the danger pass.

For matchless speed and beauty and pride of blood and bone
The bushmen of the Border had marked us as their own.
All day they planned their stockyards and set their blue-gum bars,
All night they wrought our capture as they dreamed beneath the stars.

THE OUTLAW

They tracked us to our playgrounds. They hid to watch us feed.
They matched their weighted walers against our naked speed;
And when we broke and beat them, out-wiled them, and out-ran,
I was the proud grey stallion that thundered in the van!

For long our speed defied them. We met and beat their best:
The Border's swiftest horses and the picked men of the West;
But Drought rode down the ranges and drove us, worn and weak,
From out the sheltering mulga to the flats beside the creek.

Then with their corn-fed horses they chased us, frail and afraid,
And forced us foamed and fretting to the yards that they had made;
Within their ten-foot fences and behind their blue-gum bars
They held us—kings of freedom whose fence had been the stars.

They broke my mares to harness. They saddled my splendid sons
To round the cattle on drafting-camps on drought-bound western runs.
These they bent to their bidding; but I was aware and awake;
They broke my sons to service, but me they could not break!

I threw their famous riders one by one as they came:
The lean, brown reckless bushmen that sought my heart to tame.

THE OUTLAW

I would not bear their burden, I who had never borne
More than the dust of the noonday, more than the wind of the morn!

And then he came—my master! Lissome and iron-thighed,
Lord of the earth's wild horses, riding as Centaurs ride.
Boldly I battled beneath him; I matched my strength with his own.
I had thrown a hundred riders. He was not born to be thrown

He scored my ribs with greenhide. He spurred my flanks till they bled.
He checked my mouth with the bar-bit till the foam came back to him red.
I fought like a maddened wild-cat at the ceaseless sting of his steel,
I turned like a tortured tiger-snake and bit at his rowelled heel.

I gave him no easy triumph. Stubborn, I would not yield
Till my eyes were hot and clouded and my hide was wet and wealed;
But at last my sinews slackened, my proud, wild spirit was spent,
And I bent to the will of my rider as I never before had bent.

THE OUTLAW

Then did he show no mercy, but for every stroke I had made
Struck me again, and fiercely, with his splendid strength for blade.
He spurred me out to the ranges then, dripping with blood and foam;
And weary and blind and conquered, he flogged me bitterly home.

Day after day he rode me. I ceased from the useless fight;
I could not face his courage and I could not match his might.
I had marshalled in vain my cunning, I had pitted my strength and failed,
And under the eye of the master at each new dawn I quailed.

But the fire at my heart kept burning. At last, as he stooped for a girth,
I leapt with a scream of fury and struck my foe to the earth.
I trod and trampled him under, I tore his breast with my teeth,
My towering weight above him and his quivering flesh beneath!

Then I broke to the open ranges; there was none could stop me or stay,
No creek in flood could foil me, no fence could bar my way.
I tore his trappings from me on the boughs of the belar
And, naked as I left them, I went back to wind and star!

THE OUTLAW

The scrubs were gay as ever and the lignum swamps as green,
I found the shady wilgas where our noonday camps had been.
But the Bush was still and lonely; I had neither breed nor bride,
When I whinnied down the ranges it was echo that replied.

Then came my fear upon me; a fear that fills my breast;
A racking, ruthless terror that robs me of my rest;
A shadow-shape that meets me where the wilga-shadows stir,
The phantom of a horseman that rides with whip and spur.

My flanks are cleansed of blood-marks, my bit-torn mouth is healed,
But again I meet my master and again he makes me yield.
Beneath the moons of midnight and through the morning haze
He flogs me, wet and trembling, down the old remembered ways.

I could not throw him, living, in my fierceness and my faith;
And to-day I find no courage that will rid me of his wraith.
With lean ribs lashed by terror, with flanks that fear makes red
I carry through the ranges the Unrelenting Dead.

I feed not in the daytime. At night I take no rest.
The sweat is on my shoulder and the foam is on my breast.
I bear no bit nor bridle, but 'neath the open sky
The wraith of him that rode me shall ride me till I die!

The Pack Horse

My hoofs were hid by the dew-wet clover,
  The tops of the blue-grass touched my girth,
From the river-timber a wind came over,
  Sweet with the scents of the warm, wet earth—
The day that our team to the Westward started,
  And the plains like an ocean of hope unrolled
To the gaze of the youthful, happy-hearted
Riders bent on a road uncharted
    Into the land of gold.

The way was glad with their careless laughter,
  The Bush was gay with our camp-bell's call;
The blue of the sky was our nearest rafter,
  The edge of the world was our closest wall.
I tugged, as I went, at the tall swamp-grasses;
  The hobbles clinked and the tin-ware rang.
Youth's are the eyes with the rose-hued glasses;
Youth's is the faith that never passes;
    Blithely the riders sang.

THE PACK HORSE

Sang of the girls they had left behind them;
 Sang of the gold that their toil would win;
Of the arms of the Bush flung wide to wind them,
 Of the sky and the stars that would gather them in.
Tossing their bits, the hacks went swinging;
 And proud I stepped 'neath the picks and pans,
Glad of the help my strength was bringing,
Glad, as I heard my masters singing,
        Every word was a man's.

The way was long to the western ridges;
 Summer was swifter than horses' feet;
Behind us, we knew, were our broken bridges
 Where the pools had dried in the dust and heat.
Sick for the sun like a blood-fed spider
 Over the web of the world to pass,
Slower we stepped with the pack and the rider,
And every night our bells went wider,
        Searching in vain for grass.

We came at last to the sand-swept spaces;
 A mountain of quartz stood rugged and white,
The men were famished, with drawn, grey faces;
 Our ribs were lean and our flanks were light;

THE PACK HORSE

But there—all pink at the day's beginning—
  Was the spot that the rose-hued glass had shown;
There, at their feet for its worthless winning,
Heart of sorrow and soul of sinning,
        Gold, they might take and own.

They left their picks to the wind and weather,
  Yet I carried more than my back could bear,
And I was their hope, for my mates together
  Lay lean and dead on the drift out there.
Bravely I staggered beneath my loading,
  But drought had stolen my strength away,
I could not travel for all their goading;
At night I knew with a grim foreboding
        Death would come with the day.

The dawn looked down on a pack-horse dying,
  And a load that lay in the grey-white dust,
And a haggard horseman, "He cannot," crying,
  And another cursing, "He must. He must."
One struck with a rope. The sky went reeling;
  A tiny cloud in the East turned red.
When sense to my stricken brain came stealing,
I knew that one on the sand was kneeling,
        And that one lay dead.

THE PACK HORSE

I did not die. When I saw him going,
 I rose to my feet and, faint and weak,
Followed; and so, untold, unknowing,
 We came at last to the one full creek;
And so through the windswept desert spaces
 Back to the pasture-lands of pine,
Back to the world of girths and traces,
With a secret hid from the searching faces—
 His secret and mine.

The White Ibis

When the fierce Barwon from the Border brings
   His massed battalions to the drought's defeat,
Above his pathway, with white folded wings,
   I dream in the noon's heat.

I hear the Southward gallopers go by,
   Bearing the message of the brown flood's threat;
I hear the whistling teal above me fly
   With glistening wings and wet.

I see the ruins of a hundred farms
   With plunder of grey banks beneath me swept;
I know the dawn's fear and the night's alarms,
   I know the vain watch kept.

Sometimes there passes with the drifting things,
   Lifting and falling, turned to the blank sky,
A drowned face whiter than my snow white wings,
   Then—a lone mourner—I,

THE WHITE IBIS

Who know the deep heart of the Barwon best,
   And all the hunger of his hate unfed,
Pluck, in my pity, from my snowy breast
   One white plume for the dead.

Cicadas

When the Bush is still as death,
And the night wind whispers under her breath,
When the white stars beckon without a word
And not one leaf of the box is stirred—
Sudden, as though at the baton-fall
  Of a hidden leader, the oak-trees break
Into sibilant music, one and all;
  And every pine has a harp to wake,
And every gidyea a tune to call.

Then the bridle-path that was dumb and drear
Rings with an elfin music clear,
And the shimmering starlight wraps us round
With a cloak of passion, a robe of sound.
We pierce the shadows with watchful eyes;
  But, however the moon shine bold and bright,
However the weird notes fall and rise,
  There is never a sweet-throat singer in sight
'Twixt the sombre earth and the silver skies.

CICADAS

'Tis a song of love and a song of pride,
And it swells in a rolling splendid tide,
Till the night with its rosy warmth is lit
And the cold grey Bush is a-throb with it.
Then suddenly swift, as it were a sword
   Had flashed from some jealous angel's hand,
And severed the music's silken cord,
   Cloaked Silence stoops on the listening land,
With the broken bowl of her peace restored.

Sydney

The green Bush mantles your shoulder,
   The blue wave washes your feet;
There be greater cities and older,
   But never a city so sweet.
By gardens sloped to the water,
   By clean towers built for pride,
You were born for an Empire's daughter,
   And bred for an ocean's bride!

By every sun-browned maiden
   That laughs on your low sea-beach,
By your tanned Apollos laden
   With all that your long waves teach,
By each clasp in your diamond splendour,
   By each kiss in your leafy cove,
You were made for the passionate tender
   Embrace and avowal of love!

SYDNEY

By the banks of your rippling river,
  And the camping-grounds in the trees,
You were made for ever and ever
  For love and laughter and ease.
For sunlit oars on the water,
  For soft hands trailed in the foam,
For a moon on the heeling quarter,
  When the white sea-wings come home!

Not a ship that rocks in your fairway,
  Not a liner lashed to your quays,
Not a war-gig chained to your stairway
  But has brought from the outmost seas
Some heart that will soon grow tender
  To your charms of beach and grove,
And go sadly forth from your splendour
  As a lover would leave his love!

A Bush Night

I remember the tilt of the deep canvas chairs, and the men sitting idle,
And out in the paddock a hoof going past and the click of a bridle,
And everywhere else the weird silence that lay upon sandhill and clearing,
Till the hum of a questing mosquito beat loud like a drum on our hearing.
I remember the pale summer lightning that flashed on the purple horizon,
Full-sweep like the sword-play of giants, the dark to bedeck and bedizen
With gold for the path of the planets; and far by the creek I remember
A red fire that leapt and lay down, and died out in disconsolate ember:
The camp of some lonely wayfarer. The heat of the night hovered o'er us;
Then loud from the marge of the distant lagoon came the clamouring chorus

A BUSH NIGHT

Of bull-frogs that moaned to a waterless sky for the rain cloud denied them.
Shrivelled and shamed stood the sunflowers, and prayed to the shadows to hide them.
The stars like cut gems in the darkness above the dim pepper-tree twinkled,
And somewhere beyond the burnt sandhill a cowbell incessantly tinkled.
The heat laid a garment about us, no wind set the vine leaves a-quiver
That fenced the broad-boarded verandah, no breeze blown across from the river
Brought coolness or comfort or promise; the bull-frogs ceased suddenly singing;
Then sounded the creek of a cane chair, and one from among us up-springing
Woke the wide boards with a jangle of loose-buckled spur-rowels trailing,
And clanked to the water-bag hung from the roof by the vine-trellised railing,
Clinked the tin pannikin, dipped it, and holding it brimmingly lofted,
Murmured, "The Lord send us rain and fat horses!" then tipped up and quaffed it.

The Australian Fleet

Long and long has she slumbered, till many a mouth denied
There was life in the ancient spirit that folded our fathers' pride,
Till many a lip grew scornful and curled at a nation's name
That could borrow our island honour and trade upon England's fame.

Long was her pride in awaking, this Queen of the Southron Seas,
Slow has she been in making a flag to fling to the breeze;
But at last, alert and stirring, she has heard what the sagas sing—
At last the wheels are whirring, the hammer and anvil ring.

Could the old bold blood run calmly, could the old quick pulse beat slow
While the long waves leap on the Leeuwin and winds on the Otway blow?
Hark to the ocean crooning the old, old song made new:
"Come to me, Sea King's children—my warm wide breast for you!"

THE AUSTRALIAN FLEET

They have left their fires in the ranges, they have left their ploughs on the plain,
They have left their colts in the stockyard, to come to their own again!
To plough with their keels the furrows their fathers ploughed of yore,
To fasten the sea's white horses to the yoke of the oak once more!

What fear for the nameless future? What doubt for the years unrolled?
If the hands are new to the labour, is the blood not tried and old?
Shall not the spirit of Nelson, of Grenville, and Howe and Drake
Look down on these decks of venture and guard them for England's sake?

Black Wings

Sextons of the Overland! Buriers of the dead,
Where graves are lone and shallow and winding sheets are red!
Wardens of the waggon track, watchers by the creek,
Loiterers in the lignum where the blacksoil traps the weak!

Feasters at the wayside, guests at the lagoon,
Gloating over dead sheep rotting in the noon!
Robbers on the red roads, highwaymen of Drought,
Settlers of the issue that the dawn has left in doubt!

Was there ever team-horse from the chains let go,
Was there ever lean steer lightened of the bow,
But your hungry vanguard drifting from the sky
Croaked beside his shoulder, glad to watch him die?

Ever tramped our cattle knee-deep in the grass,
But you soared above them praying Death to pass?
Ever went our sheep-mobs starvedly and slow,
But you marked their weaklings stumbling to and fro?

BLACK WINGS

Ever trod a bushman, tramp, or pioneer,
O'er the plains of Famine, through the scrubs of Fear,
But darker than his danger, closer than his dread,
Shadows on his pathway, flapped ye overhead?

Call to mind the stock routes north and west and east!—
Every heap of white bones fashioned you a feast!
Call to mind the sandhills!—every wrinkled hide
Made your perch at banquet the day a dumb beast died!

Surely, at God's muster, when our mobs again
Trample through the star-grass up the purple plain,
When from creek and sandhill crowd our western dead,
He shall suffer only white wings overhead!

The Team Bullock

The sunrays scorched like furnace fires;
   The sagging wool-bales dipped and swung;
The sand poured off the four-inch tyres;
   The dust upon the float-rails clung.
   With lowered head and lolling tongue
The lead-ox leaned against the bow,
   With yoke that creaked and chain that rung
To every hoof that lifted slow.

Grim Drought had bound the Western land.
   The swamps were dry. The creek was low.
The team that dragged across the sand
   Laid wasted necks against the bow;
   And as they staggered to and fro,
Mere skeletons of bone and hide,
   The ribs that you might count a-row
Made red the chain on either side.

THE TEAM BULLOCK

Three flaring dawns had seen them yoked,
   Three scorching noons had watched them pass,
With slaver on their lips—half-choked—
   Since they had drunk or tasted grass.
   The sun bit like a burning-glass.
The near-side leader tripped and fell.
   "They're done!" said Bunt. "The thing's a farce;
An' drivin' steers is worse than hell!"

He threw his team whip on the sand,
   And, turning to the blood-red West,
He called on God with lifted hand
   To witness he had done his best;
   Then cursed the sandhills, base and crest,
The stranded waggon and the wool
   And raving like a man possessed
Thrice cursed himself for Fortune's fool.

So, blasphemous, he sought the spot
   Where lay the leader; loosed his bow,
And muttered "He's the best I've got
   And, blast him, he's the first to go!"
   He kicked its ribs with steel-shod toe,
Then freed its mate and swung the rest,
   A staggering line with heads bent low,
Along the highway of the West.

THE TEAM BULLOCK

Their hope was dead; their strength was spent;
　The leader lost who held them straight.
Dispirited and dull they went
　Beneath the pitiless yokes of Fate.
　No whip could mend their lifeless gait,
No curse could steer them out or in;
　Death on the sandhill seemed to wait,
To claim those victims gaunt and thin.

Old Warrior watched the dust go by,
　And heard the bellowing and the blows,
The drone of wheels in distance die,
　The prescient clamour of the crows.
　Then with an effort he up-rose
And, reeling like a beast in a dream,
　With drooping loins and dragging toes
Went stumbling on behind the team.

The weary bullocks heard his tread
　And stopped beside the slackened chain,
While Warrior gauntly stalked ahead
　And backed into his place again.
　Touched by a faith beyond his ken,
Bunt murmured with the reverent fear
　That comes at times to brutish men,
"My God! But that's the gamest steer!"

THE TEAM BULLOCK

He let the threatening whip-thong fall
   Along the sand, a fangless snake;
Though each ignored the starting-call,
   He could not flog—for Warrior's sake.
   With heart it seemed must burst or break
He threw himself on suppliant knees—
   "My God, upon me pity take,
For I have taken none on these!"

Black Trackers

Swart bloodhounds of the fenceless West,
  Black gallopers that lead the Law,
To whom your victims stand confessed
  By every lightest line they draw;
The hawks that high above you sail
  Have eyes less keen to pierce the blue,
The dingo on his hunting trail
  Runs slacker in the chase than you!

Your naked fathers, seeking food
  By signs upon the sand grew wise,
And tracked their quarry till it stood,
  And bore it home, a hard-won prize.
Now, clothed and horsed and paid in gold,
  Ye ride across the selfsame sands
To track the outlaw to his hold
  And leave him in his foeman's hands!

BLACK TRACKERS

With head upon your horse's mane,
  With eyes intent on every clue,
By swamp and river, ridge and plain,
  Ye follow as the Fates pursue.
Behind you, blood on spur and heel
  And foam on chain and rein and ring,
With hands that tighten on their steel,
  Ride fast the troopers of the King!

The killer's threat is in your eyes,
  The falconer's and the hunter's pride;
Athwart your brow a vengeance lies,
  Unborrowed from the band ye guide.
The hate that shaped your fathers' spears.
  The wrath that armed some ancient sire,
The blood-lust of a thousand years
  Comes back to fan your hearts to fire!

Yet I have seen your passion sleep,
  Your hate and lust and anger die,
When, stirred by human love as deep
  As ever moved a mother's sigh,
Ye rode upon a gentler trail
  And followed, through the scrubland wild,
In sorrow that ye scorned to veil,
  The footprints of a lost bush child!

Coo-ee

Foam that feeds the Leeuwin,
  Rollers in the Bight,
Cliff and sand of Coogee,
  South Head's lifting light!
Coo-ee! Coo-oo-ee!
  Hear us call to-night,
    Coo-oo-oo-ee!

Ferry boats to Manly
  Funnel-deep in spray,
Homes above the Harbour,
  Lights in Double Bay!
Coo-ee! Coo-oo-ee!
  Friends of far away,
    Coo-oo-oo-ee!

Shady road to Springwood,
  Laughing Leura Fall,
Blue Katoomba Valley,
  Grey Kanimbla wall!
Coo-ee! Coo-oo-ee!
  Hear your lovers call,
    Coo-oo-oo-ee!

COO-EE

Stars above the gum trees,
   Camp fires in the bend,
Hoofs upon the sandhills,
   And every hoof a friend!
Coo-ee! Coo-oo-ee!
   All our love we send,
      Coo-oo-oo-ee!

Blue-eyed maiden waiting
   By your slip-rail bar,
Brown-faced comrade riding
   West by sun and star!
Coo-ee! Coo-oo-ee!
   Hear us from afar,
      Coo-oo-oo-ee!

Wide the seas between us,
   Long the leagues that lie;
If no voice can voyage them
   And no voice reply,
Coo-ee! Coo-oo-ee!
   Heart to heart can cry:
      Coo-oo-oo-ee!

Comrades

Do the shearers still go riding up the Warrego to work,
Where the Thurulgoona woolshed flashes silver in the sun?
Are the bullock teams still bending through the coolibahs to
    Bourke?
Is there racing at Enngonia? Is Belalie still a run?
Do the Diamantina cattle still come down by Barringun?

Is the black soil just as sticky? Is the mulga just as dense?
Are the boys still rounding cattle on the red Mulkitty plains?
Are there still some brumbies running on the Maranoa fence?
Still some horsemen always ready with more gallantry than
    brains
To race them through the thickest scrub with loose and flapping
    reins?

Does the flood-wrack still go rocking round the barren box-
    tree bends?
Do scorching winds still steal the grass that means dear life to
    you?
Do you still receive the message that a ravished Border sends

COMRADES

Of "Water done all down the road, and starved stock coming
 through"?
Does Drought still ride by Hungerford and Death by the Paroo?

Heigh-ho! But those were battle days, and hungry days, and
 hard;
With carcases and bones picked bare at every turning met,
Lean steers upon the cattle-camps, lean horses in the yard,
And weariness and bitterness, and toil and dust and sweat!
Good luck to you, brave comrades, who are battling with them
 yet!

The Bush

I hear you slighted often and maligned,
Mis-read, misquoted, by the careless throng,
And made the home of horror and despair.
    *   *   *   *
I know your days of sorrow; one by one
Have I not gathered them into my breast
And held them weeping? But I also know
Your days of royal gladness, when the sun
Leaps like a shining herald from the sky
To call to love and laughter, and your nights
Made mellow with the shrill cicada's hum
And hung with whiter and with nearer stars
Than any of God's nights; these things I know,
And here beyond the dim dividing seas
I stand and pledge your beauty; and I ask
For you a future full of wider peace
And homesteads harbouring a nation's strength,
Oh! great warm-armed large-hearted Mother o' Men!

Steeds of the Mist

Steeds of the Mist

Steeds, O Steeds of the morning mist,
Whose halters none but the wind may twist,
Whose soft white flanks may feel no spur
But the breeze that is setting the woods a-stir;
O beautiful, silent steeds of grey,
I will give you my heart to carry away!

As I stoop in the curve of your arching manes
I shall feel the tug of your silver reins;
I shall feel the foam on your rosy breasts
As the dawn dips under your splendid crests,
Though I know that your step is firm and fleet
I shall hear no sound of your gliding feet!

You shall carry me over the mountain bar
To the land where your breeding pastures are,
Beyond where your squadrons blind the sun,
To the fields where the glittering moon-mists run,
To the forge where your hoofs are silver-shod
'Neath the anvil sparks of the stars of God!

STEEDS OF THE MIST

O beautiful, silent steeds of grey,
You shall carry my wistful heart away;
As your shadows are lost on the mountain wall
So the shadow of grief from my heart shall fall,
And the peace of the skies shall be mine to share
When you cover my heart from its world of care!

The Whaup

This is the lark of the hilltops,
  This is the mountain swallow,
This is the carrier pigeon of the joy and grief of the moor;
There is no wind of Heaven,
  No wind that he will not follow,
No height that he dare not climb on his brown wings wide and sure.

All day, all day in the silence
  He cries to the moorland places,
All day to the grey stone dykes and the peat haggs and the moss,
All day to the red grouse feeding,
  To the hares, and the shy blackfaces
Dotting the darkened glen where the slow ghost shadows cross.

He keeps no tryst in the meadow;
  He leaves the plough to the plover,
His song is not for the village or the trodden roads of the vale,
But, wheeling above the bracken,
  He has dim old words to discover
And wed to a witching music and weave in a haunting wail.

THE WHAUP

Climb from the oatfields upward
 And wait by the moorland wall,
Just where the last plough faltered: and there where the first
 heath flames
 You shall hear him, priest of the purple,
 Out of the past recall
Songs of the hills of silence and their dim forgotten names!

The Ingleside

When the shadows downward glide
Fancy rules the ingleside,
And within the glowing fire
Lie the dream fields of Desire.

Brighter than the lighted lamps
Gleam the stars on far-off camps,
Warmer than the pine-log glow
Wait the lips of long ago.

There is not a lover fair
But her face is pictured there,
There is not a comrade true
But goes redly riding through.

There is ne'er a dream of fame
But takes shape in yonder flame,
There is ne'er a song of love
But is sung in yon red grove.

THE INGLESIDE

Soft and grey a cinder falls:
Camp and grove and castle walls
Fade away in dust and flame
With our dreams of love and fame;

Yet, when shadows downward glide
Fancy rules the ingleside,
And we find amid the fire
Dream flowers of the old Desire.

The Horseman

My song is of the Horseman—who woke the world's unrest,
To slake a King's ambition or serve a maid's behest;
Who bore aloft the love-gage and reaped the rich reward;
Who swayed the purple banner and swung the golden sword!

My song is of the Horseman! steel wrist and iron thigh,
In whatsoever saddle, beneath whatever sky!
Who breaks the road for Empire; who leads the hope forlorn:
Who rides with whip and knee-pad; who rides with rope and
    horn!

My song is of the Horseman who backs the outpost law,
Who holds with helm and carbine the frontier thieves in awe!
My song is of the trooper who stands across the street,
In hours of our forgetfulness, to stay the wild mob's feet!

My song is of the Horseman who rides, unblanched, the vale;
Who dares the deepest river and risks the stoutest rail!
Who, 'neath the roaring race-stand, rides down to fence or fall;
Who bends above the boar-spear; who drives the dancing ball!

THE HORSEMAN

My song is of all Horsemen! The centaurs of all time,
Who stole for us the freedom of colts of every clime!
Who wore the spurs of mastery, who held the reins of pride,
Who left the world a heritage of sons to rule and ride!

Up! Swear by bit and saddlecloth, by crupper, cinch and horn,
The spurs our grandsires buckled by our sons' sons shall be
    worn!
Let oil, nor steam, nor wings of dream deprive us of our own—
The wide world for a kingdom and the saddle for a throne!

The Signpost

On my green grass plot I stand aloof
  Where the four white roads have met,
And I hear the tap of the coacher's hoof
  And the hum of the landaulette.
I point the road with a stretching arm,
  And the tale of the miles I tell
To duke and squire and man of the farm
  And tattered tramp as well.

I'll show you the way to Lythamstoke,
  I'll show you the way to Sheen,
The road that takes you to Burton's Oak
  And the road to Tyndal Green;
And if you are looking for Foldingfleet
  Or Lipcomb or Lilfordlea,
You have only to stand where the four roads meet
  And read of the way from me.

THE SIGNPOST

In summer the green oak twines a crown
   To hang on my half-hid brow;
In winter days when the leaves are down
   I am tapped by a windy bough.
And if there are hours when the glad wheels drone
   And the racing road-cars glance,
There are long, long nights when I dream alone
   While the mist and the moonbeams dance.

Beneath my arms have the lovers met
   In the dusk of the summer green;
I remember a lad from Hummerset
   And a maid who came from Sheen.
The hours went by and they took no heed
   Till the glow-worms lit the loam,
And the dark came down and they could not read
   The miles they were each from home.

I am friend of the gipsies, maid and man,
   And the horse with the broken knees,
And the lurcher dog, and the caravan,
   And the camp fire under the trees;
The children wild as a woodland fawn,
   The girl with the loose black hair—
I have sped them all at the grey of dawn
   Down the road to Lipcomb Fair.

THE SIGNPOST

But dearest the day when the foxhounds meet
  On my grass plot green and wide,
When the pack comes up from Foldingfleet
  And the field from every side,
When I hear the far-off hounds in flight
  And the distant horn all day,
Till the parting horsemen call "Good-night!"
  As I send them each his way.

The roads are white, and the roads are brown,
  And the roses bloom and die;
The oak-buds break and the leaves come down,
  But apart and aloof am I.
The wheels may come and the wheels may go
  With the moods of the changing year,
But white with the dust or white with snow
  I stand at the cross roads here.

I'll show you the way to Lythamstoke,
  I'll show you the way to Sheen,
The road that takes you to Burton's Oak
  And the road to Tyndal Green;
And if you are looking for Foldingfleet
  Or Lipcomb or Lilfordlea,
You have only to stand where the four roads meet
  And ask of the way from me!

A Song of the Poets

Bridges, Abercrombie, Davies,
    Yeats, and Noyes—ye favoured few!
Music of the merle and mavis
    Echoing in the song of you!
Watson, wrapped in purple splendour;
    Newbolt, nursing England's pride;
Kipling, proud, majestic, tender;
    Masefield, from the worldways wide!
Poets, while in days of weeping
    Lost Romance is mourned as dead;
Yours the gold torch, yours the keeping
    Of the old fires fanned and fed!

When the wheels of commerce, whirring,
    Still the harp and drown the lyre,
And the world's warm pulse is stirring
    To the throb of new desire;
While the feet of fashion trample
    On the heart of him who sings,
Time shall trust your brave example
    As ye sweep your golden strings!

A SONG OF THE POETS

Here and there some soul shall listen
    To your message faint but clear;
Cheeks shall glow and eyes shall glisten,
    Doubting hearts take hope for fear!

Sing, ye seers, in pride and splendour!
    Sing, ye bards, of love and life!
Tune your lyres to music tender,
    Blow your trumpet-calls to strife!
Bare the truth, the hope, the wonder,
    Point the wild-flower in the grass,
Light the glory, loose the thunder,
    Pluck the robes of those that pass!
Say the wan world still holds beauty,
    Say Romance is not yet dead!
Yours the torch is; yours the duty
    That the fires be fanned and fed!

The Gipsy

"Now cross my hand with silver" said the gipsy crone to me,
"And I will tell your life that's past and all your life to be!"
I said, "The old I know too well, and fret not for the new;
But there are many magic things I'd liefer learn from you!

O tell me what the stars have told your quiet camps at night!
What letters on the dark unrolled your fires' red fingers write!
And tell me why the willows weep, and what the larches croon
When their boughs are crossed with silver by the bonny harvest
    moon!

And tell me where the white roads lead that lure you on and on,
And why the day grows dark indeed when once your wheels
    are gone!
And tell me why I miss you so, and why my wild heart grieves
For you that come like buds in spring and go like autumn
    leaves!

O tell me what your horses drink with moon-dew from the
    grass!
O tell me when your low fires blink how close the fairies pass!

THE GIPSY

And tell me—this I most would know—what lore as babes you learn
That gives you life-long freedom of the fir-wood and the fern!

When all the night unstirred and still, waits for his lone 'Tu-whoo!'
Ah! tell me what the secret is the brown owl trusts to you!
And, when the faint red fills the East, and gold rides up the day,
What word is in the wind of dawn that sings your wheels away!

I'll cross your hand with silver if you'll tell me all I'd know
Of what the roads have told you, and the birds, and winds that blow!
Yes, tanned and wrinkled Romany, my sage and seer confessed,
I'll cross your hand with silver if you'll give me of your best!"

The Flying Scotsman

'Tis ten o'clock at King's Cross. A green flag flicks the air;
The couplings tighten link by link to take their equal share.
A London engine whistles shrill, but he—he has no need;
The distant signal drops an arm and calls him to his speed.

He slides across the jarring points on rails all wet with rain,
And flings his grey locks to the wind and sniffs the north again.
He knows the road to Scotland, where far those white rails shine,
And swift on wheels of thunder he takes the open line.

A slow train hangs beside him, drops back, and dies away;
The little trains of London, what paltry lives have they!
What know they of the glory of flinging back at speed
Each mile of the green counties between the Thames and Tweed!

The grey suburban stations hold out their lifted names,
A painted roofbeam flashes, a golden flower-bed flames;
We have no time to heed them, to pity or admire;
Between the sleepy platforms our wheels go by like fire.

THE FLYING SCOTSMAN

By field and fold and coppice he lifts his gathering power
By forty, fifty, fifty-five to sixty miles an hour!
The drowsy cattle moving slow, knee-deep in English grass,
Lift lazy heads in wonder as they watch his splendour pass.

A moment's pause at Grantham, as a bird might pause a-wing,
Then forward to the fields again, a throbbing, living thing.
O'er Midland fen and meadow, o'er Yorkshire down and dale,
Till through the mist the minster towers rise splendid from
    the vale.

Once more the brakes are lifted, and on by Durham's spires
He answers, as a horse the spur, his banked and burdened fires,
Till through the gritty coal dust the high-set house roofs shine
And swift and dark beneath us rolls down the ravished Tyne.

Clean fields again; bent toilers that poise their hoes and wait
To watch the Flying Scotsman picking up his sixty gait.
Then Cheviot shields the Lowlands with his warden majesty,
And over Holy Island comes a breath of open sea.

Where here a castle glimmers, or there a coastal town,
The whistle warns a crossing, or screams a signal down,
Till sea-gulls by the Border Bridge stoop to our slowing speed
And dip a silver wing to us to wave us home to Tweed!

Last Night

Last night I heard as in a dream,
Before the Dawn's first rosy beam,
A seagull cry
As he passed by.

There was no other bird awake;
All were yet silent in the brake,
Beneath the eaves,
And in the leaves.

What brought this lonely wanderer by,
Before a bird was in the sky,
While, breathing deep,
The world did sleep?

Through the dim veil of Night saw he
The glimmer of white foam at sea,
Or hear the roar
Of the waves' war?

LAST NIGHT

Or, flying to some point inland,
Sought he the ploughman's curt command;
The mouldboard's gleam;
The trampling team?

Half dreaming, half awake, I heard
The low call of the ocean bird;
And knew that Day
Was on the way.

And knew that God kept still in mind
Seedtime and harvest, horse, and hind,
And His great Deep
That knows not sleep.

The Carpet of the Wind

In the deep of the woodland places
   The wind a carpet weaves,
And into the pattern laces
   The gold and red of the leaves.

There has never a cloth so splendid
   By mortal brain been planned;
The colours the wind has blended
   Were fashioned in Fairyland.

What forms shall its splendour carry?
   What feet shall its fairness tread?
What love and what laughter tarry
   In the loop of its gold and red?

And the voice of the high wind answers:
   "I have woven the woodland o'er,
That the feet of a thousand dancers
   May dance on a golden floor;

THE CARPET OF THE WIND

"That, as far as my carpet covers,
  The glades may be softly trod
By the feet of the little lovers
  That walk in the woods of God."

Celandine

You blossom in no garden fair
  To glad the eyes of knight and dame,
Yet humbly with your beauty rare
  You set the roadside banks aflame.

The ploughboy turning with his team
  Upon the headland high above,
Attracted by your modest gleam,
  Shall pick you for his lady-love.

The vagrant child that tramps the road
  On shoeless feet, begrimed with dirt,
Shall gather you, a golden load,
  And lay you in her tattered skirt.

Thus do ye serve the humble need,
  Dear blossoms of the bank and glen,
That scatter gold upon the mead
  And joy within the hearts of men!

Laughter

Lend us Laughter, O gods, for our life is but vain;
We are bruised by its rods, we are galled by its chain.
What doth patience avail, or the strength to endure
In the fight where we fail? Only Laughter is sure!

Faith is comrade no more. Sorrow sees us and nods.
From your generous store give us Laughter, O gods;
That with sword of it girt, and with helm of it crowned,
We may battle unhurt, we may wander unbound!

Send us Laughter, great lords, for our woes are too deep
To be served by the swords save of Laughter or Sleep!
Lend us Laughter, O gods, and the world is our own,
From the cloud to the clods, from the cot to the throne!

It shall soften the sting of the whips that are whirled,
And a balm it shall bring for the wounds of the world.
It shall lighten the rods, it shall cover the sore;
Send us Laughter, O gods, for our armour of war!

Again

Ain't it good to see again
Leaf an' bud an' bee again—
   Friends a fellow knows!
Ain't it good to feel again
Hook an' rod an' reel again
   Where the ripple flows!
Ain't it grand to hear again
Larks a-singing clear again,
To know that Summer's near again
   An' pinnin' on her rose!

Ain't it good to find again
Winter's left behind again,
   Summer's ridin' in!
Ain't it good to pass again
Blue things in the grass again,
   Gold things on the whin!
Ain't it sweet to smell again
South winds off the fell again,
Sailin' in to tell again
   Tales of where they've bin!

AGAIN

Ain't it rare to rove again
Through the light an' love again,
 The colour an' the call!
Ain't it good to take again
Life for life's own sake again,
 Lettin' trouble fall!
Ain't it grand to know again
Seasons come an' go again,
Springtides ebb an' flow again,
 An' God is over all!

By Candle-Light

I went with my love by candle-light through the deep of the
    poplar grove;
The moon looked down on the silver leaves and I looked down
    on my love.
It is here where the shadows linger; it is here where the great
    moths are
And a moth will come to a candle-light that is tired of chasing
    a star.

We scarce could follow by candle-light the turf path wet with
    dew;
"Can you see where you're going, dear heart?" I asked. "No,
    dearie," she said; "can you?"
But the candle shone like a guiding star held high at her golden
    head;
"Your feet are so light on the grass, dear love, that you might
    be a moth!" I said.

BY CANDLE-LIGHT

Her laugh came back through the poplar leaves. A dim wing fluttered the flame.
I swept the dark with a gauzy net and muttered a new moth's name.
Then both of us knelt on the dew-wet grass and bent o'er a captured prize,
And I saw by the flickering candle-light the love-light wake in her eyes.

The kiss that I took was by candle-light in a shadow-and-silver shine;
The night wind lifted the poplar leaves as I lifted her face to mine.
The net fell down with an open fold and the fluttering moth went free,
But the heart that I caught by candle-light went home through the dark with me.

The Garden of Night

The Night is a far spreading garden, and all through the hours
Glisten and glitter and sparkle her wonderful flowers.
First the great moon-rose full blooming, the great bed of stars
Touching with restful gold petals the woodland's dark bars;
Then arc-lights like asters that blossom in street and in square,
And lamps like primroses beyond them in planted parterre;
Great tulips of crimson that rise from the factory towers;
White lilies that droop from deep windows; all flowers, the
    Night's flowers!

Blooms on the highway that twinkle and fade like the stars,
Golden and red on the vans and the carts and the cars;
Clusters of bloom in the village, lone homesteads a-light
Decking the lawns of the darkness, the plots of the night,
Then the bright blossoms of platform and signal that shine
By the iron-paved path of the garden—the lights of the Line:
The gold flowers of comfort and caution; the buds of dull red,
Sombre with warning; the green leaves that say "Right ahead!"

THE GARDEN OF NIGHT

Then the flowers in the harbour that low to the tide of it lean;
The lights on the port and the starboard, the red and the green,
Mixing and mingling with mast lights that move in the air,
And deck lights and wharf lights and lights upon pierhead and
    stair;
An edging of gold where a liner steals by like a thief;
The giant grey gleam of a searchlight that swings like a leaf;
And far out to seaward faint petals that flutter and fall
Against the white flower of the Lighthouse that gathers them all.

And flower-lights all golden with welcome, the lights of the inn;
And poisonous hell-flowers—the doorways that beckon to sin;
Soft vesper flowers of the churches with dark stems above;
Gold flowers of court and of cottage made one flower by love;
Beacons of windows on hillside and cliff to recall
Some wanderer lost for a season—Night's flowers, one and all!
In the street, in the lane, on the Line, on the ships and the towers,
In the windows of cottage and palace—all flowers, the Night's
    flowers!

The Mushroom Gatherers

Ere Fashion has waked to adorning,
  Ere Labour goes forth to her toil,
We are free of the Autumn morning
  To gather our cream-white spoil;
And from out of her curtain shadow
  The Dawn steps, rosy and red,
To dance through the dew-wet meadow
  Where the tents of the elves are spread!

Oh! the search and the sudden wonder,
  The cry and the eager run,
The circle of snow-white plunder
  Where yesterday grew not one!
Oh! the hush of the morning holy
  On meadow and marsh and hill,
And the basket that fills so slowly,
  And the basket that will not fill!

THE MUSHROOM GATHERERS

If you walk in the wet grass wary,
  If you move with a stealthy tread,
You may chance on a laggard fairy
  That has lain too long a-bed;
But a fold of your grey gown shaken,
  A tap of your tiny shoe.
And the white tent stands forsaken
  To roof a regret for you!

Yet, however our fortune varies,
  However our quest may prove,
We have found the gold-heart fairies
  That sleep in the tents of Love;
We have trodden the fields of pleasure,
  We have drunk of the dawn-wine sweet,
And have gathered enough of treasure
  If only our fingers meet!

The Border Harp

Lilting ballads there are that cling
Like busy bees on the purple ling;
   Every hill has a harper old
   Breaking a song from a harp of gold.
What shall the singer of new songs sing?

Every hoof on the hillside set,
All the pikes that have crossed and met
   Back in the reckless raiding time,
   The bards have taken and twined in rhyme
And—they ring on the moorland yet.

Every maid that was fair or frail
From Lammermuir to Liddesdale,
   Every man that was bold to ride
   On the Eastern march or the Solway side,
Lives on for the lyre in silk and mail.

THE BORDER HARP

Never a peel-tower, grey o' the wall,
But has wakened again at the rhymer's call,
   Till the crumbling stairways ring and reel
   To the clank of the rider's armoured heel
As he climbs to the bower and hall.

Never an abbey, roofless and bare,
But a singer has sung it in music rare,
   Calling the monks from their cloister cells,
   Bidding the long-dumb vesper bells
Tremble again on the evening air.

Ballad and story rise and ring,
Glamour is out on enchanted wing;
   Here where a thousand harpers old
   Tighten the strings of their harps of gold
What shall the singer of new songs sing?

A Little Bit of Garden

We need no crown or sceptre,
  For, now that it is Spring,
Just a little bit of garden—
  And every man's a king!

A little breadth of border,
  A little patch of grass,
Above it all the April sky
  Where soft the south winds pass.

A spade and rake for comrades,
  The smell of rain-wet mould—
And every time we turn a clod
  We turn a mint of gold!

A little bit of garden,
  With daffodils a-swing,
And tulip-flowers whose crimson flags
  Are only flown for Spring.

A LITTLE BIT OF GARDEN

Shy blossoming primroses,
  Forget-me-nots of blue,
And here a blade and there a blade
  Of green things peeping through.

Who seeks for crown or sceptre
  When every man's a king
Whose patch of cottage garden
  Has felt the feet of Spring?

A Farewell

Flowers in my fading garden,
  I have come to bid you good-bye
Before you have gone through the windy gates
  To the land where the dead leaves lie!

Roses, soft children of summer,
  I would not ask you to stay,
For the mist is low on the valley
  And the last late swallow's away!

Hollyhocks, tall and kingly;
  Asters, purple and sweet;
Harpalium, touching my shoulder;
  Lobelia, low at my feet.

You have jewelled my path with beauty,
  You have brought me a smile to keep;
Go, and the sun go with you
  To gladden your dreamless sleep!

A FAREWELL

Marigolds, marred in blooming;
　Lupins that languid lie;
Dahlias drooping beneath the frost;
　Good-bye, good-bye, and good-bye!

Not a wind shall blow in December
　Above the green earth's grave
But shall bid my heart remember
　The gifts that my garden gave!

There's a Clean Wind Blowing

There's a clean wind blowing
  Over hill-flower and peat,
Where the bell-heather's growing,
And the brown burn flowing,
And the ghost-shadows going
  Down the glen on stealthy feet.
There's a clean wind blowing,
  And the breath of it is sweet.

There's a clean wind blowing,
  And the world holds but three:
The purple peak against the sky,
  The master wind, and me.
The moor birds are tossing
  Like ships upon the sea;
There's a clean wind blowing
        Free.

THERE'S A CLEAN WIND BLOWING

There's a clean wind blowing,
  Untainted of the town,
A fair-hitting foeman
  With his glove flung down.
Will ye take his lordly challenge
  And the gauntlet that he throws,
And come forth among the heather
  Where the clean wind blows!

Sheep Country

Flame of the heather dying,
  Fires of the bracken lit,
Winds of October sighing
  Over the gold of it.

Clouds on the hill-top trailing,
  Shadows caught in the glen;
Whaups to the moorland wailing
  Sorrows unguessed of men.

Grey moor gathered beside us,
  Blue moor meeting the sky;
High peaks set to guide us,
  Low hills letting us by.

Rough-topped grey walls creeping
  Out to the grey sky-line;
Woods, and within them sleeping
  Tasselled and storm-tossed pine.

SHEEP COUNTRY

Tracks in the heath around us
    Only the sheep have trod;
Nothing to bind or bound us
    Save the wide skies of God!

The Plough

From Egypt behind my oxen with their stately step and slow
Northward and East and West I went to the desert sand and the snow;
Down through the centuries one by one, turning the clod to the shower,
Till there's never a land beneath the sun but has blossomed behind my power.

I slid through the sodden ricefields with my grunting hump-backed steers,
I turned the turf of the Tiber plain in Rome's Imperial years;
I was left in the half-drawn furrow when Cincinnatus came
Giving his farm for the Forum's stir to save his nation's name.

Over the seas to the North I went; white cliffs and a seaboard blue;
And my path was glad in the English grass as my stout red Devons drew;

THE PLOUGH

My path was glad in the English grass, for behind me rippled and curled
The corn that was life to the sailor men that sailed the ships of the world.
And later I went to the North again, and day by day drew down
A little more of the purple hills to join to my kingdom brown;
And the whaups wheeled out to the moorland, but the grey gulls stayed with me
Where the Clydesdales drummed a marching song with their feathered feet on the lea.

Then the new lands called me Westward; I found on the prairies wide
A toil to my stoutest daring and a foe to test my pride;
But I stooped my strength to the stiff black loam, and I found my labour sweet
As I loosened the soil that was trampled firm by a million buffaloes' feet.

Then further away to the Northward; outward and outward still
(But idle I crossed the Rockies, for there no plough may till!)
Till I won to the plains unending, and there on the edge of the snow
I ribbed them the fenceless wheatfields, and taught them to reap and sow.

THE PLOUGH

The sun of the Southland called me; I turned her the rich brown lines
Where her Parramatta peach-trees grow and her green Mildura vines;
I drove her cattle before me, her dust, and her dying sheep,
I painted her rich plains golden and taught her to sow and reap.

From Egypt behind my oxen with stately step and slow
I have carried your weightiest burden, ye toilers that reap and sow!
I am the Ruler, the King, and I hold the world in fee;
Sword upon sword may ring, but the triumph shall rest with me!

The Comfort of the Hills

Heart!   If you've a sorrow,
  Take it to the hills!
Lay it where the sunshine
  Cups of colour spills!
Hide it in the shadow
  Of the folding fern;
Bathe it in the coolness
  Of the brown hill burn;
Give it to the west wind,
  Blowing where it wills;
Heart!   If you've a sorrow,
  Take it to the hills!

Heart!   If you've a sorrow,
  Take it to the hills,
Where Pity crowns the silence
  And Love the loneness fills!
Bury it in bracken,
  Waving green and high,

THE COMFORT OF THE HILLS

O'er it let the heather's
  Peaceful purple lie!
Trust it to the healing
  Heaven itself distils;
Heart! If you've a sorrow,
  Take it to the hills!

The Roman Wall

The grey moor dips to the mist-blue valley;
  The valley stoops to the silver Tyne;
And here, on the edge of earth and sky,
Where the blackcock feeds and the curlews cry,
  Is the long Wall's lonely line.

Do the legions come in the night, I wonder,
  Trying to gather with ghostly hands
The stones that Time with his towering breakers
Has flung afar on these moorland acres
  Like sea-wrack flung on the Solway sands?

Do the moonbeams glint on the sheen of the eagles?
  Do the burnished helms in the starlight glow?
Is there no sound heard of the horses' feet
And the waggon-tyres on the wheel-worn street
  When the ghostly trumpets blow?

THE ROMAN WALL

Do they stand by the Wall, the cohort captains,
  And hearken, leaning on idle spears,
To the step of the grim, resistless Foeman
Who broke the triumph of Rome and Roman
  Under the heel of his trampling years?

Conquering Time!—yet he, too, took pity
  On glory thrust from its golden throne,
And a flower on the old Wall planted deep—
A wreath on the grave where the warriors sleep
  And the mindful war-gods watch their own.

See; I take for remembrance, red with ruin,
  From the Wall where the clashing vanguards met,
This bloom that the crumbling stones have cherished,
This after-flower of an Empire perished,
  To bind in my garland of rare regret!

The Shadow Dancers

When the swallow's dipping low and the cloud's above the wheat
You can see the Shadow Dancers as they pass on flying feet;
The swallow is no mate for them, so swift their sandals glance,
The South Wind or the West Wind is their partner in the dance.

They tread the fields as silently as bats on dewy wings,
They clash no merry cymbals and they clink no ankle-rings;
The wild rose sees the coming of the twilight that they cast
And lifts her blushing face to them—and Lo! the dance is past!

Not a watcher in the barley, not a listener in the wheat,
Sees a shape or hears a whisper of those twinkling shadow feet;
If they leave a fairy message will the corn remember it,
Or the poppies, or the charlock, when the evening stars are lit?

Flowers of the Frost

The sun is a king on the crest of the hill
    And the woods are aflame with his glory,
The voice of the north wind is suddenly still
    And the trees have forgotten her story;
From bank to white bank where the branches are met
    And the moss like some dame's powdered hair is,
With flashing white jewels the thorn-twigs are set,
    And the glen's in the hands of the fairies.

At the base of each bole, in the curves of the steep
    That the north wind herself never reaches,
The red leaves lie low, in a pitiful heap,
    That last June were the pride of the beeches;
There are diamonds hung on the wren's balustrade
    And the trunk where the squirrel's steep stair is;
There is silence as though earth herself were afraid
    Now the glen's in the hands of the fairies!

FLOWERS OF THE FROST

Fay and fay they shall gather when daylight is dead
   And the white moon comes questioning over,
The shadows themselves not so lightly shall tread
   As the foot of each gay little rover;
And each one shall pluck from his favourite bough
   A white bloom, as desire in him varies,
For summer gave never such blossoms as now
   Are the gift of our glen to the fairies.

Contentment

The gold leaf said to the brown:
"Let us take hands and go down
On the wind's wings, for summer is spent
And the sap runs slow;
We have served our time; let us be content,
Let us take hands and go!"

The west wind, passing them, heard
And paused. Each leaf, like a nestling bird,
Launched timidly, and was gently caught
And low to the earth's breast borne.
On the grass they lay—a brown leaf and a gold,
All the pride and glory of them come to nought
And made one with the mould.

Earth mourned; but they knew no grief,
Neither the brown nor the yellow leaf;
Even when the broom swept them to the fire,
"See," they said, "to what honour we are brought!
Are not these the grey cloaks that we sought
And the red shoes of our desire?"

Riches

I may neither sport nor feast;
   Wealth is not for me to make;
But the sun is mine, at least,
   And my blue hills none can take.
If I own no gardens fair
   I can watch the wild rose twine,
Wood and wold are mine to share
   And the hills, the hills are mine.

Though my purse can never buy
   Place to hear the diva's song,
There's a lark against the sky,
   And to me the birds belong.
Though I own no acres broad,
   Though I hold no farms in fee,
Yonder glorious hills of God
   Hold their purple arms to me.

RICHES

If my cellar lacks of wine,
  Blowing splendid from the sea
Are not all the hill-winds mine
  Brimming golden cups for me?
If my shelves of books are bare,
  Have I not the skies to read,
And the wild flowers that declare
  What is aye the cleaner creed?

Let the wealthy hoard their gold,
  Let the famous guard their wreath;
All I ask to keep and hold
  Is my path across the heath;
None my freeway to withstand,
  None my faith and me to part,
Just the winds to hold my hand
  And the hills to keep my heart!

The Brown Men

Lean men, brown men, men from overseas,
Men from all the outer world; shy and ill at ease;
'Wildered in the whirl of it where fashion's feet go down;
Big men, brown men, lost in London Town.

Men whose mighty flocks and herds thread the tussock grass;
Men who know the furthest forts that hold the Khyber Pass;
Men who sound the moose-call, whose camp-smoke, thin and blue,
Scares upon the springtime trail the travelling caribou.

Lean men from the overland with muscles saddle-bound,
Sighing for their stirrups and a league of open ground;
Hunters in the jungle, trackers through the thorn,
Lovers of the hoof-slide and the rope around the horn.

Men who made the mastery that might of Empire brings:
Men who built the barrages that bind the river-kings;
Men who built the outmost bridge and laid the furthest line,
Pilots of the loneliest ships that fly the English sign.

Lean men, brown men, men from overseas;
Men from all the outer world; shy and ill at ease;
'Wildered in the whirl of it where fashion's feet go down;
Do we know the worth of you—lost in London Town?

A Maker of Empire

A patient, honest, kindly friend
   The packhorse plodded down the years,
Content his humble life to spend
   In toil to aid the pioneers.
Before the swagman and his load,
   Before the waggon and the train,
He trampled out the rusty road
   And trod the dry road in again.

He bore the first prospector's pan,
   The first surveyor's tent and gear;
With Sturt and Mitchell led the van
   O'er plains of Doubt, through scrubs of Fear.
When foemen swarmed about the track
   The danger-circled path he kept,
And bore the blankets on his back
   Of watchful men who seldom slept.

A MAKER OF EMPIRE

In the grey dust of moving herds
　　He tugged at dawn the golden grass,
While through the mist like phantom birds
　　He saw the great white bullocks pass.
In the cool creek at noon he splashed,
　　Or drank at eve from brackish wells;
All day his swinging camp-ware clashed,
　　All night his bell among the bells.

Before the engine's throb and thrust,
　　Before the humming of the wires,
This overlander, swathed in dust,
　　Across the last dim range retires.
Yet those who know shall not forget
　　That North and Westward, rod by rod,
He saw the conquering camp-fires set
　　And broke the track an Empire trod.

A Summer Evening

Dusk o' the night comes down like wings;
  Silent are birds that the day found blithe,
The soft low breeze of evening brings
  The far-off chime of hone on scythe.

The nestling swallows beneath the eaves
  Chuckle and bubble, "Good-night, good-night;"
The midges dance on the dark elm-leaves,
  And the blade o' the moon gleams bright.

Here is a beetle goes late to bed,
  Yonder a moth that the star has called,
A wandering rook by the mirk misled,
  And a gull by the gloaming thralled.

Dusk o' the night comes down like wings;
  There is no sound heard but the beetle's drone
And the hum of a million tiny things
  That are dear to the dusk alone.

The Happy People

The Happy People

Do you know the Happy People? The really happy folk,
Who bear no woman's burden, who bend to no man's yoke?
The happy, laughing people who chase on golden ways
From starlight unto starlight the splendour of the days?

Their world is bright with butterflies, their path with daisies strewn;
They've a fairy on the rainbow and a witch astride the moon.
They have jewels in the sunbeams, they have diamonds in the dew;
They have love-songs in the south wind that were never heard by you!

No stream but bears their fancy in a boat of silver foam,
No fire but holds them in its heart towers as of ancient Rome.
Their green and gorgeous tents are spread in every tree that grows,
They dream with every daisy and rejoice with every rose.

THE HAPPY PEOPLE

If you'd know the Happy People, you must take wee dimpled
 hands
And go down among the daisies or across the shining sands,
For nowhere is there room for faith and nowhere time for
 truth
Save in that darling kingdom where the harpers harp to Youth.

A Lullaby

Lady Moon, O Lady Moon,
Here's a little sleepy girlie that must go to slumber soon!
Won't you glide across the window on your shining silver wings,
　　Won't you spare 'twixt noon and noon
　Just one tiny tender minute to this cot with baby in it,
Though I know you're O so busy with a hundred million things!

Lady Moon, O Lady Moon,
Let her see the polished buckles on your gleaming silver shoon!
　　Let her touch your diamond rings and the star-dust on
　　　your wings;
And should you bend above her—ah! but that would be a boon!—
　　And kiss her little rosy lips, how kind, O Lady Moon!

Lady Moon, O Lady Moon,
Tell her just one fairy-story that you've gathered as you go
　From the pinewoods or the snow,
From the gaily lighted cities or the stars above them strewn!
　　There's a sleepy little girlie that would like *so* much to know
　Just one little fairy-story, Lady Moon!

A LULLABY

Lady Moon, O Lady Moon,
It is late; and you're so busy with so many trysts to keep,
And our little wide-eyed babba—it is time she went to sleep!
    Kiss those cheeks that mock December
      With their roses picked in June;
    Though she's sleepy she'll remember,
      She'll remember, Lady Moon!

The Admiral

Low in his cushions, with wide blue eyes,
Our future English Admiral lies.

With loving thought has his life been planned;
He shall take his share of the sea's command.

He shall wear gold lace on his sleeve and breast
If God shall will it.—But God knows best.

In our hope and love we like to dream
Of his flag above and his fleet a-beam.

We like to think of that face aglow
With the kiss of the wind that the sailors know.

We like to fancy those baby hands
A strong man's clenched as he shouts commands.

And to dream of those wide blue eyes a-shine
As his ships come up in a long grey line.

THE ADMIRAL

And to picture the pride that will flush his cheek
When the terrible guns of his squadron speak.

And we love to think he will mould and make
Seamen and gunners for England's sake.

Which shall it be, when his hour draws nigh,
That his guns must break and his flags out-fly.

Germany, Italy, France or Spain?
Russia? Japan? Or the Dutch again?

Dear little Admiral, low he lies
Searching the years with his wide blue eyes.

Is he keeping a wonderful watch and ward
Over the hilt of that far-off sword?

Ah! The tides go East and the tides go West,
And life is an ocean. And God knows best!

The Bringer of Days

There are far places where she plays,
And unguessed paths down which she strays;
   And once, round-eyed, she said to me:
"The postman brings the days!

Monday he brings for me an' you,
An' Saturday, an' Thursday too,
   He brings them in his bag, you see,
An' every one is new!"

Of course! 'Twas I that had not thought
How very much the postman brought
   Besides just news, and joys, and tears,
And bills he never ought!

Ah! Postie, with that kindly smile
You've hidden long a heart of guile!
   The blame of the swift-footed years
Was yours, then, all the while?

Three

Up at seven and down the stair
To find that the sun is already there,
That the grass is green and the sky is blue
And the fir tree fringed with morning dew,
And all the world a kingdom free
With gates flung wide to a child of Three!

Down to the lane where a light wind blows
And the foxglove nods and the cranesbill grows,
Berries of red in the roses' place,
Feathery grasses that fan your face,
Bluebells brushing a naked knee—
O, but the world is bright at Three!

An hour and an hour and the sun goes down;
The rabbit is feeding, a bundle of brown;
The swallows are crossing the window blind;
There's a star in front and a star behind,
And creeping shadows by every tree—
And O, but the days are short at Three!

Baby's Trumpet

When Baby blows her trumpet
  The elves of mischief ride,
Her eyes are lit with laughter,
  Her cheeks are puffed with pride.
What gift of cradle-fairies
  Has taught our queen to know
God's angel guards are waiting
  To hear her trumpet blow?

When Baby blows her trumpet
  The tramp of feet one hears,
One sees her loyal legions
  With sunlit lifted spears;
Their golden breastplates quiver,
  Their golden helmets shine,
When Baby blows her trumpet
  And wheels her troops in line.

BABY'S TRUMPET

When Baby blows her trumpet
  The world grows young again,
The silent aisles of Fancy
  Grow loud with marching men.
Before her deathless army
  The earth is all her own,
No rival ranks are marshalled,
  No answering bugles blown.

When Baby blows her trumpet
  The woods of Wonder wake,
The hills of Hope are peopled
  With swords for Some One's sake.
From every windy tree-top,
  From every peak above,
In splendour fly unfolded
  The crimson flags of Love.

When Baby blows her trumpet
  The kingdoms cease from sound;
To rule so rich an army
  No empress yet was crowned.
Earth's towers shall yield their treasure,
  Earth's gates fall back unbarred,
When Baby with her trumpet
  Calls up her golden guard.

The Grey Nurse

At the feet of this oldest of nurses,
  Whom the wind has made grey with his strife.
Happy youth in its wonder rehearses
  The play and the labour of life;
And there for our children the ocean,
  Robed round with the charm of her spells,
Turns over with tireless devotion
  Her treasure of seaweed and shells.

She fills their rock-gardens with blossom,
  She smoothes the clean sand for their feet,
And tells them, clasped close to her bosom,
  Old tales that are tender and sweet;
Old stories, old sagas and verses,
  Old ballads of beautiful tears,
Whose words are the tender grey nurse's,
  Whose tune is the sob of the years.

THE GREY NURSE

We forgive her her squadrons of thunder,
  Her gauntleted hand on the gate,
Her long years of rapine and plunder,
  Her ages of anger and hate,
As we watch her chase, romping and eager,
  The bare feet all browned by the sun,
Over castles her love will beleaguer
  And trenches her joy will o'er-run.

We have watched her, a war-queen, in splendour,
  Come riding in harness of spray;
We have seen her soft-mantled and tender
  Lean low to our babes in the bay;
And, forgetting her sword-play and slaughter,
  When the little white wavelets are curled,
We know the wild Witch of the Water
  Is the gentlest grey nurse in the world.

The Burning of Summer

I heard a laugh in the leafless trees;
  I saw on the path of the open sky,
Borne by the light October breeze,
  A blue smoke drifting by.

A tiny maid in her waltz of cheer
  Paused as she heard my rustling tread:
"Come and help at our dancing, dear; ,
  We are burning Summer!" she said.

The heap grew higher. The white smoke rose,
  The glow of the fire a memory brought.
It is only the heart of a child that knows
  How to laugh when a summer is burned, I thought.

A Song of the Rain

The rain swept over the hill,
  The rain fell steep in the street.
Said the yeoman, "I cannot till!"
  Said the lovers, "We cannot meet!"

Still the Rain King rode in power,
  Setting his storm-clouds free,
Nursing the fruit and the flower,
  Tending the lawn and the lea!

"But I cannot play," sobbed the child
  "My daisies are all so wet!"
And the Rain King, hearing, smiled,
  But his heart grew full with regret.

He has stalled his steed in the West;
  He has gathered his clouds away.
"Lovers may sorrow and toilers rest,
  But the children," he said, "must play!"

The Bundle in the Shawl

In all the sorrow of the street
  That surges round us like a sea,
In all the pity of bare feet,
  In all the pain of poverty,
There seems to me no sadder sight
  Or one that more the heart appals
Than mothers shielding from the night
  The bundles in their tattered shawls.

Here some poor wretch to honour lost
  Hastes with her babe Hell's draught to buy,
Its little patient cold arms crossed
  Where only happy arms should lie;
And here some other, spent and weak,
  Has stumbled forth at duty's call,
Close holding to her breast and cheek
  The bundle in the tattered shawl.

THE BUNDLE IN THE SHAWL

Fair innocence of hope bereft,
  Pale youth where youth is but a name,
Sons bound to slavery or theft,
  Dear daughters doomed to toil or shame;
Poor hapless babes, the wind blows cold
  Through that poor mantle thin and torn,
But were it trebled, fold on fold,
  It would not cover you from scorn!

Man's pity hath not entered in
  To help the broken and the weak;
The breasts ye suck are seared with sin,
  Or sorrow blinds the eyes ye seek!
There are those others clothed in silk,
  But suffering's bitterness of gall
Is fed you in your mothers' milk,
  Poor bundles in the tattered shawl!

The old must suffer as they may
  What fate or fault hath bid them bear,
But thorn and steepness of the way
  Must these, the little children, share?
For pity of the mother-love
  That through the ages throbs and calls
May angels fold their wings above
  The bundles in the tattered shawls!

To My Baby Girl

O little heart
That beats so close to mine,
I pray for you
That every heart be true
Which through the years shall worship at your shrine;
May none betray,
None kneeling with his roses give you rue;
This only, little heart, I pray,
I pray for you.

In the Woods

The North winds blow with a promise of snow
  And grey is the Autumn sky,
But merry and warm through the woods we go,
  Neddy and Babs and I.

Babs is wrapped in her scarlet shawl
  And snug in her basket chair,
And Daddies of course don't matter at all,
  And Neddy's all right in his hair.

Neddy that walks with the stately stride
  Of a race that has carried kings,
Taking the Babs for a "booful ride"
  That she wouldn't exchange for wings!

We follow the path through the copses brown
  Where the shadows hide like thieves,
And the sound we hear like a silken gown
  Is Neddy's hoofs in the leaves.

The bracken is bronze and white and gold,
  The mosses are wet and green.
The drops that the bending fern-fronds hold
  Are the pearliest ever seen.

IN THE WOODS

Fluttering down comes a red, red leaf;
  Perhaps from the big beech-tree
A fairy is dropping her handkerchief
  To Neddy and Babs and me!

And now we stop while the dead leaves stir
  And a step so light goes by
That it might be a pheasant under the fir
  Or a raindrop out of the sky!

And now we stand while a red-brown head
  Plays hide-and-seek with three—
A squirrel trying to trick old Ned
  And baffle my Babs and me!

But the sun is gone, and the shadows creep,
  And the gold lights flicker and flee;
And Daddies must work and Neddies sleep
  And Babses take their tea.

So we wave one arm to the darkening firs,
  And one to the sunset sky,
And home we go—my hand in hers—
  Neddy, and Babs, and I.

The Witches' Steeds

There are four steeds that the witches ride
Down the starry meadows shining and wide:
You can hear them snort as they gallop through,
Tugging their bridles of roped pearl-dew,
But never a one can be seen by you!

One is the North Wind; grey tne sky
When he bites at the beeches, cantering by.
Hark to his madcap rider rate
As she plucks at his forelock: "Straight! Go straight!"

One is the East Wind; four elf-grooms
Fed him all day with the first Spring blooms;
But the country lasses, a-tired o' their Maying,
Hear him, still starved, in the night-time neighing.

The West Wind, mad with his witch's spur,
Plunges and leaps, but he can't throw her!
And the children turn in their sleep and wonder
When they hear his hoofs on the house-top thunder.

THE WITCHES' STEEDS

The South Wind last; behind him the leaves
And the swallows come home to our English eaves.
Oh! he lifts each hoof so light and so light
That there's never a flower in the still warm night
That is crushed by the whinnying South Wind's flight.

The Barring of the Gates

"Then there aren't any fairies at all, Mummy?"

The Fairy King lies dead—Ring, ring the bluebells over him!
Gather the beech leaves red for a winding sheet to cover him!
There will be no more dancing down in the woodland hall—
And there never were fairies at all, dear heart,
There never were fairies at all!

What hand hath drawn the bars on the golden gates so soon?
Who told you of stars just stars, and a moon-face only a moon?
There will be no more riches hid where the rainbows fall—
And there never were fairies at all, dear heart,
There never were fairies at all!

You will not sleep to-night, dear, waking and wondering why
Out on their broomsticks bright, dear, no witches ride in the sky!
Why do your child-lips tremble, why do your big tears fall?—
For there never were fairies at all, dear heart,
There never were fairies at all!

THE BARRING OF THE GATES

Even when we have grown old, dear, they bar us our gates of bliss,
Hiding the hands we would hold, dear, taking the lips we would kiss,
Till we doubt in the dreary midnights that thrill to a dead year's call—
If there ever were fairies at all, dear heart,
If there ever were fairies at all!

The Storks

There's a quaint old Nor'land fancy and a legend that I love,
  Of the white storks winging Southward through the mist;
Of a palace or a cottage that they fold their wings above
  Laying baby in his cradle to be kissed;
Of their building on the house-tops and the nests by no one stirred
  For the love-gift of the little lives they bring;
Of the children's wide-eyed wonder at the great white drifting bird
  That has borne them in the shadow of his wing.

Was it flying thus, I wonder, through God's blue and sunlit aisles,
  With the silent snows of Norway spread below,
That the babies caught the witching, merry sunlight of their smiles,
  And the pureness of their hearts as white as snow!
Call it fairy-tale or fancy, 'tis a legend strangely sweet,
  And a clinging hand, a little upturned mouth,
Always sets me dreaming, dreaming that I hear the wings a-beat
  Of the white storks flying softly to the South.

War

A Dream of England

     I dreamed a dream
Of some great Empire arming for a fray;
Of fond farewells and parting words to say,
And strong men torn 'twixt love and battle-pride,
Taking, soft-eyed, their women's last bequest
With clinging mouth to mouth and breast to breast—
Then to the gangway proudly; and I guessed
     That this was England!

     Then in my dream
I saw an army of the bravest brave
Flung back and forward in the battle's chance,
Its flag upon the leaguered city wave,
Its dusty worn battalions still advance.
I saw the bodies of its leaders strew
The mountain passes as it blundered through
Without a thought of wavering; and I knew
     That this was England!

A DREAM OF ENGLAND

      And dreaming still,
I saw a lurking ambush in the thorn,
A sleeping camp, an outpost strangled, then
A little force surprised and overborne,
A little force of brave out-numbered men
That had no time to fight, no wish to flee:
Ranged by their jammed gun, standing knee to knee
With folded arms; until it seemed to me,
      This must be England!

      Last, in my dream
I heard far-off among green Island lanes
In farm and cot and manor the one cry
"Fight on! Fight on! More troopships and more trains!"
And in my dream the soldiers crowded by!
I saw waved hands and heard the cheers that sped,
Drowning the wailing for the Island dead,
And turning in my sleep I woke and said:—
      "This is our England!"

War

War! The winds are sighing it,
The hill birds are crying it
  To the valley's uttermost bounds.
River and burn repeat
The noise of the hurrying feet
  Of the unleashed hounds!

War! The bridles are jingling,
Noble and yeoman mingling,
  At the summoning bugle's call.
Proudly the English muster;
The pennons of Ireland cluster;
  Scots, be up with them all!

Rise, as ye rose aforetime,
Bonneted, busked for war-time,
  Grim as ye grouped of yore!
By the bloody fields ye have trodden—
Waterloo—Badajoz—Flodden—
  Who be your masters in war?

WAR

By the squares ye have held unshaken;
By the forts ye have stormed and taken;
  By your charging, resolute Greys;
By Dargai Height; by Delhi Gate;
Now stand ye to the swords of Fate
  As ye stood in the olden days!

Heroes laurelled of all renown
Look from their high Valhalla down,
  Trusting the swords they bred;
Sons of such that have gone before—
Kings in valour and Lords of War—
  Go where their stars have led!

Play up, pipers of Scotland, blare to the world that waits!
Tell them our youth and manhood stand massed by the Northern Gates!
Tell them our three joined kingdoms are fain for the battle to be;
Tell them the heart of Scotland is the readiest heart of the three!

A Song of the Old Men

Youth! To you is the splendid prize:
  To have left your school but a term or two,
And to sudden see with your shining eyes
  The path of honour made plain for you;
To be picked at once for the Game of Games,
  To be called to a quest that the soul bestirs;
To fling your torch on the altar flames,
  And ride with the Great Adventurers!

Pity us, Youth!—If our feet be slow,
  If our eyes that watch you be old and dim,
Our hopes go forth on the road you go,
  Our hearts are chanting your battle hymn;
And whether your fate be a grave in France,
  Or a laurel wreath and the Golden Spurs,
What would we give for your chance, your chance
  To ride with the Great Adventurers!

The Stragglers

Under the blue of wide heavens in the haze of the Western heat,
The sweating horses go blindly down the golden lanes of wheat,
Till, over the drone of the reaper, and over the clink of the
  chains,
And the cry of a startled prairie bird that flits to the further
  plains,
Comes a whispered sound on the sea-wind sighing;
And the jingling harness is hushed, and hushed is the reaper's
  hum;
The bugle call comes nearer, and nearer the throb of the
  drum!
Hark to the West, the lonely West, the loyal West replying:—
  "Mother, we hear your crying,
  Mother, we come!"

Dark in the driving dust-wrack the wild mob wheels and rings;
Yonder the spurred flank reddens, yonder the foam-fleck flings;
Till, over the snort of the camp horse, and over the tramp of the
  hoofs,
And over the din of the dust storm that rattles the iron roofs,

THE STRAGGLERS

Comes a whispered sound on the sea-wind sighing;
And the tramp of the cattle is hushed, and the weird cicadas' hum,
The bugle call comes nearer, and nearer the throb of the drum!
Hark to the Bush, the drought-bound Bush, the brave old Bush replying:—
        "Mother, we hear your crying,
        Mother, we come!"

The Channel Guard

Where runs the Channel East and West
  A stout troop holds the way,
With helms that bear a snow-white crest
  And riding-cloaks of grey;
Beneath the winds that rule their reins
  The proud-maned horses prance,
Rough-ridden down the misty lanes
  'Twixt Dover Cliffs and France.

We hear at night the troopers grey
  When, touching English ground,
They tap upon our doors to say—
  "All's well; so sleep ye sound!
All's well; our bridle chains are bright,
  Our swords unsheathed and keen,
And, late or early come the fight,
  Our squadrons stand between!"

THE CHANNEL GUARD

They will not fail, this faithful band;
  Their hearts with ours are twined;
Their strength is Britain's to command;
  To her their swords are signed.
They broke of old the Spaniard's boast
  And stayed his fleet's advance,
These riders by the Dover Coast
  Who hold the roads to France.

Sure sentinels that never sleep
  They guard us night and day—
Our restless troopers of the deep,
  Our grim patrols in grey.
So long as yonder Channel waves
  Before our gates remain,
The Despot and his driven slaves
  May watch the Straits in vain.

A Begging Song for Belgium

Here's a beggar, here's a gipsy, here's a tramp
  With the dust of Flanders travel on his feet;
Here's a soldier from a still unconquered camp,
  Coming limping through the hazes and the heat,
With a story of a hope was never lost,
  Of a courage that was never trampled down,
Of a corner that the foe has never crossed,
  Of a king with nought but honour for a crown!

Here's a story, here's a legend, here's a tale
  That will sink into the heart of you and sear:
Of the homeless on their seaward-pointed trail,
  Of the exiles too much broken for a tear;
Of the old men bent and wearied by the way,
  Of the women looking back upon their dead,
Of the young men vowing vengeance on the day,
  Of the children crying bitterly for bread!

A BEGGING SONG FOR BELGIUM

Here's the season, here's the moment, here's the chance
    To show that hearts in England still can beat
For such men as manned the guns that saved us France,
    For such men as will not recognise defeat,
For the country that the foeman has betrayed,
    For the women he dishonoured to his shame!—
Shall your gold not be by seventy times repaid
    If you give it now for Belgium in God's name?

The Unawakened Hills

Here, in the unawakened hills,
  From shepherds' cots that lonely lie
In quiet glens by peat-fed rills
  The blue smoke trails upon the sky,
Unblown by any wind of war,
  By any breeze of hate unstirred,
While half the world is fighting for
  A treaty torn, a broken word!

The shepherds walk their hirsels wide
  And reck not of the wrath of kings,
And watch the hawks above them glide
  And see no wraith of darker wings.
The women watch the moon-mist rise
  And gather greyly in the fern,
Yet dream not of the distant skies
  On which the flames of battle burn!

THE UNAWAKENED HILLS

A fox across the glidders steals,
   A grouse cock sounds his raucous call,
A whaup above the moorland wheels,
   A grey-hen watches from the wall;
The bracken flames in chrome and red,
   In golden plumes the grasses dance—
O, hills unwakened!—and the Dead
   Lie sleeping in the fields of France!

The Ladies from Hell

(The German nickname for the Highlanders)

The battle sways backward and forward
  In wedges and hollows and curves,
A hard-pressed battalion is yielding,
  A leader has called for reserves.
Hark! Drone of the pipes in the distance
  That grows to a soul-stirring swell!
Brown-skirted, with bonnets a-bobbing,
  Come up the gay Ladies from Hell!

O brightly the sunlight is gleaming
  On the blades that the rifles reveal.
The Ladies are wearing their jewels;
  Hurrah! for the glint of the steel!
O fiercely they swing to the music,
  Their faces alight with its spell;
Brave-hearted, bare-kneed and triumphant,
  The lean-featured Ladies from Hell!

THE LADIES FROM HELL

Our foes have made war upon women
   By dastardly choice of their own.
The daughters of Belgium are weeping.
   The mothers of Flanders make moan.
Ho! Slayers of maids and of mothers,
   Do your bayonets serve you as well
When you're called up to stand in the open
   And face the grim Ladies from Hell?

O Weeping Glens

O weeping glens; O mountain peaks that mourn
   For youth and valour destined to the day,
Who shall give back your sons thus roughly torn
   From your hurt breasts; those men that marched away?

O cornfields green from the sowing; O meadows lush
   From the first laugh of Spring; O woods where the doves
Low in the dim-lit fir-boughs and the hush,
   Heedless of man's new madness, nurse their loves!

Who shall give back your gallant ones, your best;
   Sure hand to the plough, strong arm to the scythe;
Him who swung the axe longest without rest;
   Him whose song in the morning sounded most blithe?

Scotland! dear Mother of the Brave! In vain
   Thou callest through the dawning and the mirk
To those beloved that will not come again—
   Those noble sons dead by their nobler work!

The Scots Greys

O "terrible grey horses" that woke Napoleon's fears,
The thunder of your beating hoofs makes music down the years!
At Blenheim and at Ramillies your fires of glory grew
To blaze upon a watching world, full-flamed, at Waterloo!
And still our fathers tells their sons in many a Nor'land town
Of how their grandsires in the Greys rode the French standards down!

O "terrible grey horses," the Russians heard your tread
When Scarlett's men, at one to ten, rode up the lanes of lead!
The burghers saw your bridle-chains shine silver in the sun
When French spurred into Kimberley to say the siege was done!
And now by Mons and Charleroi, by Meaux and Compiegne,
The spirit fed at Fontenoy has fired your troops again!

The men that once opposed your march with rifle, trench, and sword,
Are fighting on your flank to-day to stem the vandal horde.
The spirit of your country calls, ye need no whip nor spur
To gallop 'neath the gauntlet-hands that hold the world for her.
Charge on, and break them, gallant Greys! your grim name keep and hold
O "terrible grey horses" that Napoleon feared of old!

The Colours

In this dim Cathedral place
  Hang the banners of our land:
Riven banners of the race
  Made to conquer and command!
Where those age-old colours twine,
  Faded, torn, and stained with red,
Scotland in her inmost shrine
  Keeps the memory of her Dead.

Scotland's banners! Who shall gaze
  On their faded folds unstirred?
Who in these Imperial days
  Hear unthrilled their martial word?
Down the High Street cheer on cheer!
  Hark! the trampling troops go by!—
Banners in the dimness here
  Taught such soldiers how to die.

THE COLOURS

Scotsman! In the silence kneel!
   To these emblems lift thine eyes!
Here in God's own presence feel
   Right's insistent victory lies!
By those tattered flags and torn,
   By that sacred purple stain,
Scotland's banners shall be borne,
   Conquering, by her sons again!

Remounts

In the rosy red of the dawning your hoofs on the roadway ring,
You that shall carry our heroes, you that shall fight for the King,
You that shall lead the triumph in a last long trampling line
When the swords have saved us Europe and slashed their way
 to the Rhine!

Called from an Irish farmyard, called from an English fen,
Called from a prairie pasture to measure the lives of men,
What courage that laughs at danger, what spirit that scoffs at
 Death
But, born to our Empire freedom, ye have drunk with your
 every breath!

Bred in our conquering kingdoms, you too are the Empire's sons,
You that shall tug at the waggons, you that shall gallop the guns,
You that are part of our glory, whose help has the years bestowed
Whenever our grandsires gathered, wherever our fathers rode!

REMOUNTS

And, faith, ye shall never fail us when the whimpering bullets
 fly,
When the lances shiver and splinter and Death in his spurs goes
 by;
When the stricken reels in his saddle and the chill hand drops
 the rein,
And bloody out of the battle ye wheel to the tents again!

Hail to the hero that waits you; gunner, hussar, or dragoon!
Hail to the day of your glory—and the War-God send it soon!
Luck to your prancing squadron whose hoofs on the roadway
 ring!
Proud ye shall carry the victors who carry the swords of the
 King!

The Heroes

There came a west wind swinging
  Through their silver myall trees,
To the quiet bushland bringing
  Clash of world-wide destinies.
From their Southron sun-dreams waking
  Swift they rose and buckled sword,
Their Imperial burden taking
    At the first flung word!

To their high ideals turning,
  Unto great adventure cast,
In the veins of each leapt burning
  Britain's proud and splendid Past!
In their gold hearts hid the glory
  That is Britain's crowning grace
Long as Fame repeats the story
    Of the Island Race!

THE HEROES

At the word they rose and gathered
    Down the dusty western roads,
Where the struggling teams, foam-lathered,
    Strain before the ten-ton loads.
Where the darkling pine scrubs feather;
    Where by creeks the bell birds call;
Rode they, knee and knee together,
        Lithe and lean and tall!

Farm and camp and cattle station
    Gave their dearest sons that day—
"If you need them, Mother-Nation,
    Take them!" mother hearts could say.
Ports where quay sides clattered loudly,
    Cities crowned with tower and hall,
Gave their best, and gave them proudly
        At the Empire's call!

By the storied Nile we found them,
    Free of wizard Egypt's gift,
Tombs of ages piled around them,
    Sands of Time their ceaseless drift;
Found them ever southward turning
    To one star above the sea,
Since it woke their nightly yearning
        For the grass countree.

THE HEROES

Once again the transports bore them
    Eager to an unknown coast.
Honour's flag flew white before them,
    Pride flung pennons o'er their host.
Broke the dawn of their endeavour
    Down the Turkish hilltops grey.—
For the land that bred them, never
        Broke a prouder day!

Time shall tell that splendid story
    Of the beaches swept by Death,
Of Australia's crowning glory
    Wafted on the war-guns' breath!
Far Australian lands shall name them
    With a new Imperial pride,
Glad in after years to claim them
        As their sons who died!

Sails of Victory

Where the lone look-outs their night-watch keep,
   Where the quivering searchlights gleam,
Comes up like a bird on the guarded deep
   A ship of the Seas of Dream.

A ship with a fighting crew complete—
   Three decked, full sailed and sparred—
A ship that is not of the North Sea Fleet
   Nor yet of the Channel guard.

O grey patrols of the grey North Sea,
   Ye may wheel and let her through,
For the flag at her foremast flying free
   Is the old Red, White, and Blue!

Admirals all, your pennons dip
   As proudly astern ye stand!—
This is the *Victory,* Nelson's ship,
   Come back to her old command!

A Song of the Flag

There's a flag the free winds follow—'tis the banner England bought her
    With the mastery of the main;
Every ship upon its azure has a lion to support her,
It is barred with every sunbeam 'twixt the wind-cloud and the water,
It is starred with faith and freedom, and it bears on every quarter
    Broken galley-bench and chain.

There's a flag the blue waves dip to—on the turret-ship and trader,
    On the liner out and home;
Every crown upon that banner has a conquering name to braid her,
Every rose in every corner has a limbered gun to shade her,
And the Admirals of England chase the Spaniard's doomed Armada
    Round its borders in white foam.

A SONG OF THE FLAG

It has hailed a thousand summers since we haltered the white stallions
        In their blue fields running free;
Since we forced them to our bidding, ramping royal-maned battalions,
Bearing down our swift three deckers on the treasure-laden galleons,
Or, scarce mouthing at their bridles, arching crests in courtly dallianee
        With our keels upon the sea.

Through the gates our hands flung open sail the fleets of all the Powers
        Dipping flags as they go past,
All the flags of all the nations like a bunch of coloured flowers,
'Mid the flags of every nation not a prouder flag than ours
As she dips a royal answer from a hundred fortress-towers
        Each a stronger than the last.

We have won it with the yew bow, we have held it with the yeoman,
        We have fostered it and fed;
With a lion-crest above it as a boast and battle-omen
We have built this wider Empire than the widest of the Roman,
Built it safe and built it surely on the bodies of our foemen
        And the bones of English dead.

A SONG OF THE FLAG

Dead we left upon the ranges with the bloodwoods arching over;
    Dead we left in Maori fern;
In the shadow of the kopjes where the vultures wheel and hover;
In the jungle; in the backwoods with the maple-leaves to cover;
Dead, amid the ocean dirges, laid beside their deep-sea lover
    Shrouded, leaded, dropped astern.

Dead we buried with their honours, with their medals laid beside them
    To the roll of the dulled drum;
Dead that fell above their axes with the rites of Death denied them,
Dead we heaped within the trenches with a shallow ridge to hide them,
With our banner for a grave-cloth that the English flag may guide them,
    Through the unknown dark to come.

Gallant, gallant dead of England! To the wandering winds that know them
    Let us flaunt our flag afar.
On the hills that guard our heroes, on the fenceless seas below them
It is ours to hold the Empire that they left us, ours to show them
We shall not forget the homage and the honour that we owe them
    Who have made us what we are!

A SONG OF THE FLAG

Though the roses of the banquet red and white are round us lying,
        And the sparkling wine-cups foam,
Though the lissom jewelled dancers all their witching arts are plying
With a heaving of white bosoms and a soft seductive sighing,
With our heel upon the dead realms shall we droop among the dying
        Like a lost Imperial Rome?

We, who never failed a summons from the feasting to the foray
        When the foe stood threatening by,
We, who gave our best so bravely; we, who bought so dear our glory,
Shall we trample on our laurels? They are stained with sweat, and gory
But, laid safe between the pages of our Book of Empire story
        They shall shine when roses die.

By the English blood that bought it! 'tis a kingdom worth the keeping!
        'Tis a royal priceless ward!
Though our halls have vacant places, though our mothers' hearts go weeping,

A SONG OF THE FLAG

When we hear the bugles calling, when the naked blades are leaping,
All the world shall know that England, if she slept was only sleeping
        With a hand upon her sword!

God of Battles! If we served Thee as a smiter to Thy smitten,
        If we fought as true men fight,
Hear our prayer, O God of Battles! Let the light we bear be lit in
Every kingdom of the wide world, and across our flag be written:—
FREEDOM! BY THE GRACE OF HEAVEN AND THE GAUNTLET-HAND OF BRITAIN!
        AND MAY GOD DEFEND THE RIGHT!